This is the Fidel Castro I believe I know…. A man of austere ways and insatiable illusions, with an old-fashioned formal education, of cautious words and simple manners and incapable of conceiving any idea which is not out of the ordinary…

He has the nearly mystical conviction that the greatest achievement of the human being is the proper formation of conscience and that moral incentives, rather than material ones, are capable of changing the world and moving history forward.

I believe he is one of the greatest idealists of our time and perhaps this may be his greatest virtue, although it has also been his greatest danger.

Gabriel García Márquez

Though his father was a wealthy landowner during Fidel's childhood, he had left Spain poor, and in Cuba had sold home-made lemonade from a cart. His mother, about whom one hears little, except that she was originally his father's cook and was very religious and that Fidel adored her, probably instilled in her son a love of and belief in the poor he has never forgotten. I believe Fidel was deeply inspired by these two. They named him "Faithful" after his godfather

Few con   o.
Both wor   of
the most   or
devil. Tak

My Early Years

by
Fidel Castro

edited by Deborah Shnookal & Pedro Álvarez Tabío

OCEAN PRESS
Melbourne • New York

Cover design by David Spratt

ISBN 1-876175-07-9

First printed 1998

Printed in Australia

Published by Ocean Press
Australia: GPO Box 3279, Melbourne, Victoria 3001, Australia
• Fax: (61-3) 9372 1765 • E-mail: ocean_press@msn.com
USA: PO Box 834, Hoboken, NJ 07030 • Fax: 201-617 0203

Library of Congress Catalog Card No: 98-65906

OCEAN PRESS DISTRIBUTORS
United States: LPC/InBook,
    1436 West Randolph St, Chicago, IL 60607, USA
Canada: Marginal Distributors,
    277 George St. N., Unit 102, Peterborough, Ontario K9J 3G9
Britain and Europe: Global Book Marketing,
    38 King Street, London, WC2E 8JT, UK
Australia and New Zealand: Astam Books,
    57-61 John Street, Leichhardt, NSW 2040, Australia
Cuba and Latin America: Ocean Press,
    Calle 21 #406, Vedado, Havana, Cuba
Southern Africa: Phambili Agencies,
    PO Box 28680, Kensington 2101, Johannesburg, South Africa

Contents

Fidel Castro

Fidel Castro Ruz was born in Birán, in the former province of Oriente, on August 13, 1926. Born into a well-off landowning family, he attended elite Catholic private schools in Santiago de Cuba and Havana, and graduated from law school at the University of Havana in 1950.

While at the university, he joined a student group against political corruption. He was a member of the Cuban People's Party (also known as the Orthodox Party) in 1947 and became a leader of its left wing. That same year, he volunteered for an armed expedition against the Trujillo dictatorship in the Dominican Republic, although the expeditionaries were unable to leave Cuba to carry out their plans. As a student leader, Castro went to Venezuela, Panama and Colombia to help organize a Latin American anti-imperialist student congress to coincide with the founding conference of the U.S.-sponsored Organization of American States. While in Colombia, he participated in the April 1948 popular uprising in Bogotá.

After Fulgencio Batista's coup d'état of March 10, 1952, Castro began to organize a revolutionary organization to initiate armed insurrection against the U.S.-backed Batista dictatorship. He organized and led an unsuccessful assault on the Moncada army garrison in Santiago de Cuba on July 26, 1953, for which he and over two dozen others were captured, tried, found guilty and imprisoned. More than 60 revolutionaries were murdered by Batista's army during, and immediately after, the Moncada attack. While in prison Castro edited his defense speech from the trial into the pamphlet *History Will Absolve Me*, which was distributed in tens of thousands of copies and became the program of the July 26 Movement. Originally sentenced to 15 years, he and his comrades were released from prison after 22 months in May 1955 as a result of a growing public campaign.

On July 7, 1955, Castro left for Mexico, where he began to organize a guerrilla expedition to Cuba to launch the armed insurrection. On December 2, 1956, along with 81 other fighters, including his brother Raúl, Che Guevara, Camilo Cienfuegos, Juan Almeida and Jesús Montané, Castro reached the Cuban coast aboard the cabin cruiser *Granma*. For the next two years, Castro directed the operations of the Rebel Army, in addition to continuing as central leader of the July 26 Movement. After an initial setback, the guerrillas were able to reorganize their forces, and by late 1958 had successfully extended the struggle from the Sierra Maestra mountains throughout the island.

On January 1, 1959, Batista fled Cuba. In response to a call by Castro, hundreds of thousands of Cubans launched an insurrectionary general strike that ensured the victory of the revolution. Castro arrived triumphantly in Havana on January 8 as commander in chief of Cuba's victorious Rebel Army. On February 13, 1959, he was named prime minister, a position he held until December 1976, when he became president of the Council of State and the Council of Ministers.

He has been first secretary of the Central Committee of the Cuban Communist Party since its founding in 1965.

Fidel Castro's final school report
from Belén College, Havana, 1945

Fidel Castro Ruz
1942–1945

He always distinguished himself in all subjects related to arts and letters. An excellent student and member of the congregation, he was an outstanding athlete, always courageously and proudly defending the school's colors. He won the admiration and affection of all. He will study law, and we have no doubt that he will make a brilliant name for himself. Fidel has what it takes and will make something of himself.

CR

Preface

Dozens of biographies in many languages have been produced over the 40 years of the Cuban revolution probing the man whose "bearded face [is] one of the best-known physiognomies in the contemporary world."[1] This book is unique in that it presents the first collection of autobiographical sketches by Fidel Castro, a man who has guarded his personal life so closely, especially the period of his childhood and youth.

At the age of 26, in July 1953 Fidel Castro led a youthful group of 160 armed combatants to attack the Moncada army barracks in Santiago de Cuba, coordinated with a support action in Bayamo. The goal was to spark a popular uprising against General Batista who had seized power in a military coup on March 10, 1952. Most of the young rebels not killed in the attack were captured and tortured.

Having only graduated from law school a few years previously, Fidel Castro, who was kept in isolation for most of his time in prison, prepared his own defense. He used his courtroom appearance to argue for revolutionary change in Cuba, concluding with a defiant statement: "Condemn me. It does not matter. History will absolve me!"

Who was this young man who made such a dramatic entrance on to the stage of Cuban and subsequently international politics, a stage on which he still occupies a prominent place?

A U.S. intelligence report from around 1947 described Fidel Castro (still at university) as "a typical example of a young Cuban of good background who, because of lack of parental education or real education, may soon become a fully-fledged gangster."[2]

In this book, Fidel Castro describes his family background, his childhood, education at elite Catholic schools, and the religious and moral influences that led to his involvement in politics from an early age.

---

[1] Tad Szulc, *Fidel: A Critical Portrait*, 23
[2] Quoted by Herbert Matthews, *The Cuban Story*, 140

The book only covers the period up through his university days and the Batista coup in 1952. Castro himself has argued that his personal and political course was set by this time — prior to the attack on the Moncada garrison. "Before March 10 [Batista's coup] I had already arrived at the conviction that it was necessary to organize a revolutionary movement, and to this end I was prepared to dedicate all of my position and my resources as deputy."[3]

For this reason, *My Early Years* concentrates on Castro's formative years, providing a glimpse of Fidel, the boy and the young rebel, in his own words. He recollects his days at the University of Havana when violent gangs ruled student politics; his early thoughts about armed struggle; his travels in Latin America as an international student organizer; his participation in solidarity actions with Latin American anti-imperialist movements; his first-hand experience of a popular uprising in Colombia in 1948; and his years as a young lawyer and political activist.

Soon after the Cuban revolution in 1959, journalists and writers from everywhere flocked to the island to discover the "real" Fidel Castro by carrying off the elusive prize — an interview with the man himself. Lee Lockwood, a U.S. photo journalist, argued that "if [Castro] really is our enemy, as dangerous to us as we are told, then

---

[3] Fidel Castro interview in Lee Lockwood, *Castro's Cuba, Cuba's Fidel*, 158. This is a reference to the fact that Castro was a candidate for the elections scheduled for 1952 — elections that were aborted by Batista's coup. Writing from prison on April 2, 1954, Castro reflected on his early parliamentary candidature: "Politics is such a hoax! In my experience, even with the best of men and the best parties, it is unbearable. Now, recalling all the meetings tirelessly and fanatically attended by so many idol worshippers, who remained seated hour after hour, listening to 20 different speakers engaged in a furious oratorical competition in which all of them said the same thing ... I have come to the conclusion that our people are infinitely patient and kind. Thinking of it here in this lonely cell, I cannot understand how they applauded instead of hurling their chairs at the charlatans. All these politicians are like actors in a theater — they play their roles, earn the audience's applause, and are damned if they think of anything but election day, about which they're obsessed!

"I was one of them. I can only explain it on the basis of inexperience, the environment, and inability to do anything else when your head is full of a million ideas. I was a player in that circus. Like Archimedes, I searched for the pivot on which to move the world. Deep in my heart I was disgusted by it all; I thought I saw hypocrisy and mediocrity everywhere, and time has shown that my instincts did not deceive me." Quoted by Mario Mencía, *The Fertile Prison: Fidel Castro in Batista's Jails*, 134.

it seems obvious that we ought to know as much about him as possible... . Whether one agrees or disagrees with another, the best way to begin understanding him is by listening to what he has to say."[4]

Washington Post correspondent Lionel Martin was one of the first to focus on Castro's early years, speculating with some humor that "Fidel's law school grades for the spring semester of 1949, his senior year, presaged his life's course. He received an *outstanding* (*sobresaliente*) in labor legislation, but only a simple *pass* (*aprovechado*) in property and real estate, grades befitting a convinced socialist."[5]

A more recent flurry of biographies appeared in the late 1980s and early 1990s, in the wake of the collapse of the Soviet Union and the socialist bloc, predicting the immediate demise of Castro and revolutionary Cuba. One of the more vitriolic biographers, Georgie Anne Geyer, noted that: "[T]he world continued to define the mysterious Fidel Castro in myriad and phantasmagoric ways. He was a Third World Napoleon, the head of the first Fascist Left regime in history, a psychopathic caudillo, a socialist caudillo, Jesus Christ on earth, an aging pimp, the Lone Ranger, a socialist huckster, everydictator, everyprince, everyrevolutionary, a thwarted democrat, a Communist, a Gallego *cacique*, Machiavelli's Prince, Francisco Franco's classic guerrilla, an inquisitional bishop, a Caribbean Proteus, a new kind of actor on the world stage, a dynastic Communist, the vicar of the complexes of the Third World, the prototype of the new Third World, a classical opportunistic son-of-a-bitch... "[6] Geyer wrote Castro's epitaph as "truly the last Communist."

Bolder still was Andres Oppenheimer, whose book was titled *Castro's Final Hour: The Secret Story Behind the Coming Downfall of Communist Cuba.* "This book," wrote Oppenheimer in January 1992, "does not attempt to predict how Fidel Castro will fall, or how long his final hour may stretch. It may be a matter of weeks or... a few years."[7]

---

[4] *Castro's Cuba*, xix
[5] Lionel Martin, *The Early Fidel: Roots of Castro's Communism*, 72
[6] Georgie Anne Geyer, *Guerrilla Prince*, 391
[7] Andres Oppenheimer, *Castro's Final Hour: The Secret Story Behind the Coming Downfall of Communist Cuba*, 9

Yet somehow, Castro has survived and the people of Cuba seem to be recovering from the severe economic blows that have battered the island in recent years. Raúl Castro once remarked, "The most important feature of Fidel's character is that he will not accept defeat."[8]

Tad Szulc, author of a major biography of Castro commented, "Cuban and world history would have evolved differently had this single individual been less determined and, most importantly, less lucky. Fidel's luck is a recurrent theme of his existence."[9] As *My Early Years* shows, there were numerous occasions when the young Fidel Castro's life might have been cut short, even before the audacious attack on the Moncada garrison in 1953 and the near disaster of the *Granma* expedition from Mexico in 1956.

Political influences

Much speculation has always surrounded Fidel Castro's political evolution, in particular his relations with the Cuban Communist Party and his commitment to Marxist ideas. In an unprecedented personal dialogue with students at the University of Concepción in Chile in November 1971, during the government of President Salvador Allende, Fidel Castro discussed at length the formation of his political ideas:

> I was the son of a landowner — there was a reason for me to be a reactionary. I was educated in religious schools that were attended by the sons of the rich — another reason for being a reactionary. I lived in Cuba, in which all the films, publications and mass media were 'made in USA' — a third reason for being a reactionary. I studied at a university in which, out of thousands of students, only 30 were anti-imperialists and I was to become one of those. When I entered the university, it was as the son of a landowner and, to make matters worse, as a political illiterate.[10]

He goes on to describe how he first began to question the social system after reading "bourgeois political economy."

---

[8] Quoted by Herbert Matthews, *Castro: A Political Biography*, 29
[9] Tad Szulc, *Fidel: A Critical Portrait*, 23
[10] Fidel Castro, *Fidel in Chile: A Symbolic Meeting between Two Historical Processes*, 85

[The regular capitalist crises of overproduction were] apparently due to the inexorable, natural and unchangeable laws of society and nature; it was said that crises of overproduction will inevitably occur, bringing in their wake unemployment and starvation. Despite there being too much coal, workers will freeze and starve.

That landowner's son, who had been educated in bourgeois schools and had been subjected to Yankee propaganda, began to think that something was wrong with the system, that it didn't make much sense.[11]

Castro says he considered himself "lucky to have been the son and not the grandson of a landowner."

As the son of a rising landowner, I at least had the advantage of living in the countryside and could mix with the peasants, with the humble people, who were all my friends. As the grandson of a landowner, it is quite possible that my mother would have taken me to live in a swank neighborhood in the capital; that milieu would have encouraged selfishness and other traits.

Luckily, some of the positive factors were developed at my school: a certain idealistic rationality and a concept of good and evil — something very simple and elementary. It also developed a sense of justice; a certain spirit of rebelliousness against impositions and oppression led me to analyze human society and turned me into what I later realized was a utopian communist. At that time I still hadn't been fortunate enough to meet a communist or read a communist document.

Then one day a copy of the *Communist Manifesto* fell into my hands. I read some phrases I'll never forget, such as where it says that the bourgeoisie accuse us of wanting to abolish private property, whereas the truth is that private property has already been abolished for nine-tenths of the population and can only exist for the rest if it doesn't exist for the others....

What phrases! What truths! These truths we could see in everyday life. What truths! And these are only a sample. The part where the *Manifesto* analyzes class society and other things was like a revelation to me, a utopian communist who thought that

[11] Ibid.

the world could function in a certain way, by virtue of rationality. I had been far from being able to imagine human society as a product of evolution, a product of the laws of history, of dialectical rather than immutable laws.

When I saw the origin of human society and its class divisions, it was so convincing that it hit me like a clap of thunder, and I was won over to those ideas. However, that didn't mean I was anywhere near being a communist!

My head was full of ideas, but I didn't belong to any party. I had indoctrinated myself. I had no clear idea of what imperialism was. I still hadn't read *The State and Revolution* or *Imperialism: The Highest Stage of Capitalism* — two tremendous books by Lenin — which threw light into the forest in which I lived. The fact is, I felt like some little animal that had been born in a forest but didn't understand it. Then, all of a sudden, I came across a map of that forest, a description of the geography of that forest and everything in it. It was then that I got my bearings. Without that orientation, we wouldn't be here now, that's how correct Marx's ideas were! We just wouldn't be here!

Now then, was I a communist? No. I was a man who was lucky enough to have discovered a number of ideas and who was caught up in the whirlpool of Cuba's political crisis long before becoming a fully-fledged communist. I was already in that whirlpool before being recruited. I recruited myself and began to struggle.[12]

Fidel Castro has always insisted that he "wasn't indoctrinated by any party member, communist, socialist or extremist,"[13] but that the two major political influences on him were the works of the Cuban revolutionary hero, José Martí, and the writings of Karl Marx.

In so far as this book probes the intellectual, moral and political influences on the young Fidel Castro, it illuminates the unique character of the Cuban revolution itself, a process in which Castro played such a central role.

---

[12] Ibid., 85–87
[13] Ibid., 85

Fidel Castro and Che Guevara

The autobiographical insights in this book make it easy to imagine how an immediate rapport developed a few years later (in June 1955) between Fidel Castro and a young, intellectual rebel from a wealthy Argentine family, Ernesto Guevara. After their first meeting, Guevara decided to throw in his lot with the Cuban revolution. Che had just turned 27 and Fidel was almost 29.

"They were of the same generation, but their practical-ideological identity, which would grow even deeper with the passing time, was more important than that coincidence in linking them," reminisced Jesús Montané, a Cuban revolutionary veteran who was with Che and Fidel in Mexico. Montané describes the "fellow feeling that immediately sprang up between them," and comments that they expressed "the same personality and temperament."[14]

Recalling this first meeting, Guevara told Ricardo Masetti: "I talked with Fidel all night. By the time the sun came up, I was the doctor of his future expedition. In fact, after the experiences I'd had during my long trek through Latin America and its finale in Guatemala, I didn't need much persuading to join any revolution against a tyrant, but Fidel impressed me as an extraordinary man. He tackled and did the impossible things. He had exceptional faith that, once he left for Cuba, he would get there; once he got there, he would fight; and by fighting he would win. I shared his optimism."[15]

What developed was an extraordinary bond between two similar and yet different young men from opposite ends of the continent of Latin America.

* * * * *

The selection and editing of this book was done by Deborah Shnookal and Pedro Álvarez Tabío, director of the Publications Office of the Cuban Council of State. The editors make no claim to this book being the definitive autobiography of Fidel Castro's early years. There are many — and perhaps quite significant — gaps that remain to be filled in. It is left to the reader to decide how to assess Castro's personal reminiscences presented here.

---

[14] Jesús Montané, Preface, *Che: A Memoir by Fidel Castro*, (Ocean Press), 14–15
[15] Quoted by Montané in his preface to *Che: A Memoir by Fidel Castro*, 14

The purpose of this selection is simply to allow one of the most controversial political figures of the 20 century to speak for himself. In this regard, *My Early Years* should become an essential reference for anyone wanting to understand Fidel Castro and the Cuban revolution a little better.

The selections included in *My Early Years* are: Two excerpts from an extremely wide-ranging discussion with Brazilian priest, Frei Betto, which took place in May 1985 in Havana. Betto, a liberation theologist, took advantage of the opportunity to probe the Cuban leader on a more intimate level about his childhood and schooling, the religious and ethical influences on him and many other personal matters.

Castro, well known for resisting any attempt to publicize or commercialize his private life, surprisingly responded with remarkable candor and openness. Betto's interview, published as *Fidel and Religion*,[16] subsequently became the most comprehensive account of Castro's early years and a best-seller in many editions in several languages.

The other two pieces selected for this book are not well known, and one is published here in English for the first time.

On September 4, 1995, Fidel Castro addressed a meeting in the Aula Magna (Great Hall) of the University of Havana, where he had attended law school and began his political career. In his speech, Castro describes how, exactly 50 years before, he had entered the university as a "political illiterate," but learned quickly how to survive in an atmosphere where mafia-like gangs ran student politics.[17]

Colombian journalist Arturo Alape's interview with Fidel Castro about his experience in the popular uprising in Colombia in April 1948, often referred to as the *Bogotazo*, is published here in English for the first time.[18] This interview, conducted in September 1981, gives a picture of the young Fidel Castro's developing consciousness of the need for Latin American unity, his outstanding moral and

---

[16] *Fidel and Religion: Conversations with Frei Betto* was published in English by Ocean Press.
[17] This speech was originally published by Ocean Press in English in *Cuba at the Crossroads* by Fidel Castro.
[18] Alape's interview was published in *De los recuerdos de Fidel Castro: El Bogotazo y Hemingway* (Editora Politica, Havana, 1984)

physical courage, and his unshakable self-assurance — despite the fact that he was only 21 at the time.

The introductory essay by Gabriel García Márquez was originally published by Ocean Press in *An Encounter with Fidel* by Gianni Minà.

Our thanks to Mary Todd for her translations of the excerpts from Frei Betto's *Fidel and Religion* and Arturo Alape's interview with Fidel Castro on Colombia.

Deborah Shnookal
June 1998

A Personal Portrait of Fidel

by Gabriel García Márquez

Speaking of a foreign visitor whom he had accompanied for a week on a tour around Cuba, Fidel Castro said: "How that man can talk — he talks even more than I do!" It is enough to know Fidel Castro just a little to realize this was an exaggeration, a great exaggeration, because it is impossible to find anyone more addicted than he to the habit of conversation.

His devotion to the word is almost magical. At the beginning of the revolution, hardly a week after his triumphal entry into Havana, he spoke on television for seven hours without respite. It must be a world record. During the first few hours, the people of Havana, not yet familiar with the hypnotic power of that voice, sat down to listen in the traditional way. But as time passed, they went back to their daily routine, with one ear to their affairs and the other to the speech.

I had arrived the day before with a group of journalists from Caracas, and we started listening to the speech in our hotel rooms. Without a pause, we later continued listening in the elevator, in the taxi that took us to the business districts, on the café terraces blooming with flowers, in the freezing air-conditioned bars, and even walking down the streets where radios came full-blast through open windows. By evening we had carried out our day's schedule without missing a word.

Two things caught the attention of those of us hearing Fidel Castro for the first time. One was his terrible power to seduce his listeners; the other was the fragility of his voice. It was a hoarse voice, which at times was reduced to a breathless whisper. A doctor, on hearing the hoarseness, concluded that even without the marathon speeches that seemed to flow as long as the River Amazon, Fidel Castro was doomed to lose his voice within five years. Shortly afterwards, in August 1962, this prognosis seemed to have its first alarming confirmation when he was left mute after having made a speech announcing the nationalization of U.S. companies. But it was a transitory set-back which did not recur. Twenty-six years have passed since then. Fidel Castro has just turned 61,[1] and his voice sounds just as uncertain as ever; but it continues to be his most useful and irresistible instrument in the subtle craft of the spoken word.

Three hours, for him, are a good average for an ordinary conversation. And three hours at a time, the days speed by him. As he is not an academic leader entrenched in his offices, preferring to seek out problems wherever they may be, he can be seen in his discreet car, without the roar of accompanying motorcycles, slipping along the deserted avenues of Havana or on some out-of-the-way road at any time, even in the pre-dawn hours. All this has given rise to the legend that he is a drifting loner, a disorganized and unconventional insomniac, who may turn up for a visit at any hour and keeps his host awake until dawn.

There was some truth behind that image in the early years of the revolution, when he retained many of his habits from the Sierra Maestra. Not only because of his lengthy speeches, but because he had no real home, nor an office, for more than 15 years, nor did he have any fixed daily routine. The seat of government was wherever he might be, and power itself depended on chance, occasioned by his wanderings. Now it is quite different. Without detracting from his so characteristic impetuosity, he has finally imposed a certain order on his life. Previously, days and nights would pass with him snatching only a few winks here and there whenever exhaustion overcame him. Now he tries to allow himself a minimum of six hours' undisturbed sleep, although not even he himself knows when that might be. Depending on how things go, it could just as well be 10:00 at night or 7:00 the next morning.

He devotes several hours to routine matters in his office of the presidency of the Council of State, where there is a well-ordered desk, comfortable furniture of untanned leather and a bookshelf reflecting the breadth of his tastes: from treatises on hydroponics to romantic novels. From the half a box of cigars he used to smoke each day he became an absolute abstainer, just to have the moral authority to combat smoking in the country where Christopher Columbus discovered tobacco — still a major source of revenue for Cuba today.

The inclement ease with which he gains weight has obliged him to adhere to a permanent diet. This is an immense sacrifice, considering his large appetite and his insatiable pleasure in hunting recipes which

---

[1] This essay was written in 1987.

he likes to prepare with a kind of scientific fervor. One Sunday, letting himself go, he finished off a good-sized lunch with 18 scoops of ice-cream. However, usually he picks at a fish fillet with boiled vegetables, and then only when hunger overcomes him, rather than according to set mealtimes. He stays in excellent physical condition with a few hours of gymnastics each day and frequent swimming. He limits himself to a glass of straight whisky consumed in almost invisible sips, and he has managed to control his weakness for the spaghetti he was taught to prepare by the first papal nuncio of the revolution, Monsignor Cesare Sacchi. His Homeric but momentary rages are now a thing of the past, and he has learnt to dissipate his dark moods in an invincible patience.

In sum: an iron discipline. But in any case this is never enough, considering how the inevitable scarcity of time imposes an irregular schedule and the force of his imagination may carry him off at any moment. With him, you know where you will begin, but you never know where you will wind up. It is not unusual on any given night to find yourself flying in an airplane to some secret destination, to be best man at a wedding, fishing for lobsters on the open sea or tasting the first French cheeses made in Camagüey.

A long time ago he said: "As important as learning to work is learning to rest." But his methods of rest seem too original, and apparently do not exclude conversation. Once he left an intense work session close to midnight, with visible signs of exhaustion, and returned in the pre-dawn hours fully recovered after swimming for a couple of hours. Private parties run counter to his character, as he is one of the rare Cubans who neither sings nor dances, and the very few he does attend change in nature the moment he arrives. Perhaps he does not realize. Perhaps he is not aware of the power his presence imposes, a presence which immediately seems to fill all the space, although he is neither as tall nor as corpulent as he appears at first glance. I have seen the most self-assured people lose their poise in his company, by contriving to look composed or adopting an exaggerated air of confidence, without ever imagining that he is as intimidated as they are, and has to make the initial effort so that it is not noticed. I have always believed that the plural which he often uses when speaking of his own acts is not so majestic as it seems, but rather a poetic license to conceal his shyness.

Inevitably the dancing is interrupted, the music stops, the dinner is put off, and the crowd gathers around him to join in the conversation which begins immediately. He can remain like that for any length of time, standing up, without drinking or eating anything. Sometimes, before going to bed, he will knock very late at the door of a close friend, where he can show up unannounced, and says he's staying only five minutes. He says it with such sincerity that he does not even take a seat. Little by little, he gets stimulated again by the new conversation, and after a while he collapses into an easy chair and stretches out his legs, saying: "I feel like a new man." That is how it is: weary of talking, he rests by talking.

Once he said: "In my next reincarnation I want to be a writer." In fact, he writes well and he enjoys it, even in a moving car in the notebooks he always has at hand for writing down whatever comes to mind, or sometimes personal letters. They are notebooks of ordinary paper, bound in blue plastic, which over the years have accumulated in his private files. His handwriting is small and intricate, although at first glance it looks as simple as a schoolboy's. He approaches writing like a professional. He corrects a phrase several times, crosses it out, tries it again in the margins, and it is not unusual for him to search for the right word for days, consulting dictionaries, asking around, until he finds what he wants.

In the 1970s he fell into the habit of writing out his speeches, so slowly and with such meticulousness that they were almost mechanical. But this same virtue spoilt them. Fidel Castro's personality seemed to change when he read them: the tone was different, the style, even the quality of his voice. In immense Revolution Square, before half a million people, he several times felt himself suffocating in the strait-jacket of the written word, and every chance he got he departed from the text. On other occasions he found that his typists had made an error, and rather than correcting it as he went along he would stop speaking and make the change with a ball-point pen, taking his time. He was never satisfied. Despite his efforts to liven them up, and despite the fact that he did succeed in many cases, those captive speeches left him feeling frustrated. They said everything he wanted to say, and perhaps they said it better, but they left out the greatest stimulus of his life, which is the excitement of risk.

The improviser's stand, then, seems to be his perfect environment, although he always has to overcome an initial inhibition which few people recognize and which he does not deny. In a note he sent me a few years ago asking me to participate in some public ceremony, he said: "Try for once to get over your stage fright, as I myself must do so often." Only in very special cases does he use a card with some notes, which he unceremoniously takes out of his pocket before starting and holds within view. He always begins in a nearly inaudible voice, quite hesitant, pushing forward in the fog on an uncertain course, but seizing upon any glimmer to gain ground inch by inch, until he lashes out with something like a great paw and grabs hold of the audience. Then a give and take is established, exciting them both and creating between them a kind of dialectical complicity. In this unbearable tension lies the essence of his elation. It is inspiration: the irresistible and dazzling state of grace, which is denied only by those who have not had the glory of experiencing it.

In the beginning, public events commenced with his arrival, although that was as unpredictable as the rain. For some years now he has been arriving precisely on time, and the duration of his speech depends on the mood of the audience. The infinite speeches of the early years belong to a past now confused with legend, because so much of what had to be explained at that time is now understood, and Fidel Castro's style itself has become more compact after so many sessions of oratorical pedagogy. He has never been heard to repeat any of the papier-mâché slogans of communist scholasticism nor make any use at all of the system's ritual dialectic, a fossil language which long ago lost contact with reality and goes hand in glove with a laudatory and commemorative journalism, which seems intended to conceal rather than to explain. He is the anti-dogmatist par excellence, whose creative imagination lives hovering over the abysses of heresy. He rarely quotes the phrases of others, neither in conversation nor on the rostrum, except those of José Martí, his favorite author. He knows the 28 volumes of Martí's work thoroughly, and has had the talent to incorporate his ideas into the bloodstream of a Marxist revolution. But the essence of his own philosophy is perhaps his conviction that mass work is, above all, a matter of being concerned with each individual.

This could explain his absolute confidence in direct contact. Even the most difficult speeches seem like casual talks, like those he held with students in the courtyards of the university at the outset of the revolution. In fact, and especially outside Havana, it is not unusual for someone to call out to him from the crowd at a public meeting and a shouted dialogue will begin. He has a language for every occasion and a different form of persuasion depending on his different interlocutors, be they workers, farmers, students, scientists, politicians, writers or foreign visitors. He can reach each one at their own level with vast and varied information that allows him to move easily in any medium. But his personality is so complex and unpredictable that any one of them can form a different impression of him in the same encounter.

One thing is certain: wherever he may be, however and with whomever, Fidel Castro is there to win. I do not think anyone in this world could be a worse loser. His attitude in the face of defeat, even in the slightest events of daily life, seems to obey a private logic: he will not even admit it, and he does not have a moment's peace until he manages to invert the terms and turn it into a victory. But whatever it may be, and wherever, everything happens within the ambit of an inexhaustible conversation.

The subject can be anything, according to the interest of the audience, but often the opposite occurs when it is he who takes a single subject to all his audiences. This tends to happen during the periods in which he is exploring an idea which is bothering him, and no one can be more obsessive than he when he has set out to get to the bottom of something. There is no project, however grandiose or minute, which he does not undertake with a fierce passion, especially if he is facing adversity. Never than at such times does he look better, appear in a better mood or in higher spirits. Someone who believes he knows him once commented: "Things must be going very badly, because you look radiant."

However, a foreign visitor who met him for the first time told me a few years ago: "Fidel is getting old; last night he went back to the same subject around seven times." I pointed out to him that these almost manic reiterations are one of his ways of working. The subject of Latin America's foreign debt, for example, had arisen in his conversations for the first time some two years ago, and had been developing, branching out, growing more profound, until it became something very much like a recurrent nightmare. The first thing he said, like a simple arithmetical conclusion, was that the debt was unpayable. Little by little, during three trips I made to Havana that year, I pieced together his latest variations on the theme: the repercussions of the debt on the countries' economies, its political and social impact, its decisive influence on international relations, its providential importance for a unitary Latin American policy. Finally, he convoked a major congress of experts in Havana and gave a speech in which he left out none of the salient questions from his preceding conversations. By then he had a comprehensive vision which only the passage of time will bear out.

It seems to me that his most exceptional virtue as a politician is this faculty of discerning the evolution of a particular problem, all the way to its remotest conclusions, as if he could see not only the projecting mass of an iceberg but also the seven-eighths of it underwater. However, this faculty does not function by intuition, but rather as a result of arduous and tenacious reasoning. An assiduous interlocutor could discover the first embryo of an idea and follow its development over many months though his persistent conversation, until it is finally made public in its completed form, as happened with the foreign debt. Then, once the subject is exhausted, it is as though a vital cycle had been completed, and he files it away forever.

Such a verbal mill requires, of course, the aid of an incessant flow of information, well-chewed and digested. His supreme aid is his memory, and he uses it to the point of abuse to sustain speeches and private conversations with overwhelming reasoning and arithmetic operations of incredible speed. This task of information accumulation begins when he wakes up. He breakfasts with no less than 200 pages of news from all over the world. During the day, despite his ceaseless mobility, they pursue him everywhere with urgent information. He himself calculates that every day he has to read some 50 documents. To this must be added the reports of his official services and of his visitors, and everything that could be of interest to his infinite curiosity. Any exaggeration about this can only be approximate, such as even in the extreme case of a trip in an airplane.

He prefers not to fly, and does so only when there is no alternative. When he does fly, he is a bad passenger because of his anxiety to know everything: he neither sleeps nor reads, he hardly eats, he asks the crew for navigation maps every time he has some doubt, he makes them explain why this route is being taken and not the other one, why the noise of the turbines is changing, why the plane is bouncing in spite of the good weather. The replies, of course, must be correct, as he can discover the slightest inconsistency in a casual phrase.

Another vital source of information, of course, is books. Perhaps the aspect of Fidel Castro's personality least in keeping with the image created by his adversaries is that of being a voracious reader. No one can explain how he finds the time or what methods he uses to read so much and so quickly, although he insists that there is nothing special about it. In his cars, from the prehistoric Oldsmobile to successive Soviet Zils, up to the current Mercedes, there has always been a light for reading at night. Many times he has taken a book in the pre-dawn hours, and commented on it the following morning. He reads English, but does not speak it. In any case he prefers to read in Spanish, and at any hour is ready to read any piece of paper with letters on it that may fall into his hands. When he needs some very recent book, which has not yet been translated, he has it translated. A doctor friend sent him, as a courtesy, his treatise on orthopedics which had just been published without, of course, any pretension that he read it, but a week later he received a letter from him with a long list of observations. He is an habitual reader of economic and historical subjects. When he read the memoirs of Lee Iacocca, he discovered several such incredible errors that he sent to New York for the English version, to compare it with the Spanish. Indeed, the translator had once again confused the meaning of the word billion in the two languages. He is a good reader of literature and follows it closely. I have on my conscience having initiated him in the addiction of quick-consumption best-sellers and then keeping him up to date as an antidote to official documents.

Still, his immediate and most fruitful source of information continues to be conversation. He has the habit of quick interrogations, which resemble a *matriushka*, the Russian doll from whose interior a similar, smaller one emerges, then another, until the smallest one possible is left. He asks successive questions in instantaneous bursts until he discovers the why of the why of the final why. It is difficult for his interlocutor not to feel subjected to an inquisitorial examination. When a visitor from Latin America gave him a hasty statistic on the rice consumption of his compatriots, he did his mental calculations and said: "How strange, each one eats four pounds of rice a day." With time you learn that his master tactic is asking about things he already knows, in order to confirm his data.

And in some cases to gauge the caliber of his interlocutor, and treat them accordingly. He loses no opportunity to inform himself. Colombian President Belisario Betancur, with whom he maintained frequent telephone contact despite the fact that they had not met nor that the two countries do not have diplomatic relations, once called him about some casual matter. Fidel Castro told me afterwards: "I took advantage of the fact that we both had time to ask him for some information that did not come in the cables about the coffee situation in Colombia."

He went to few countries before the revolution, and those he has since visited on official trips he has been condemned to the narrow horizon of protocol. However, he also talks about them, and about many others he has not been to, as though he had been there. During the war in Angola he described a battle in such detail at an official reception that it was difficult to convince a European diplomat that Fidel Castro had not participated in it. The account he gave in a public speech of the capture and murder of Che Guevara, the one he gave on the storming of the Moneda Palace and the death of Salvador Allende, and the one he gave on the ravages of Hurricane Flora were great verbal images.

Spain, the land of his ancestors, is an obsession with him. His vision of Latin America in the future is the same as that of Bolívar and Martí: an integral and autonomous community capable of influencing the destiny of the world. But the country he knows most about, after Cuba, is the United States. He is thoroughly familiar with the nature of its people, its power structures, the ulterior motives of its governments, and this has helped him to steer clear of the incessant storm of the blockade. Despite the restrictions of the government of the United States there is a nearly daily flight between Havana and Miami, and not a day goes by without U.S. visitors of every kind arriving in Cuba, on special flights or in private planes.

On the eve of elections there is an incessant influx of politicians of both parties. Fidel Castro sees as many as he can see, he makes sure that they are well cared for while they wait and does everything possible to give them sufficient time for an exhaustive exchange of new information. These are veritable talk-fests. He gives them a few home truths and puts up very well with the ones they give him. He conveys the impression that nothing amuses him more than showing his true face to those who arrive prepared by enemy propaganda to meet a barbaric *caudillo*. On one occasion, before a bipartisan group of congressmen and even a Pentagon official, he gave a very realistic account of how his Galician ancestors and his Jesuit teachers infused some moral principles in him which had proved very useful in the formation of his personality. And he concluded: "I am a Christian."

It hit the table like a bombshell. The people from the United States, brought up in a culture that understands life only in black and white, skipped over his prior explanation. At the end of the visit, with the new day already dawning, the most conservative of the legislators voiced the surprising view that he believed no one could be a more effective mediator between Latin America and the United States than Fidel Castro.

Everyone who goes to Cuba hopes to have the chance to see him in whatever circumstance, although there are many who dream of a private interview, especially the foreign journalists, who never consider their work finished until they can carry away the trophy of an interview with him. I believe he would oblige them all if it were not physically impossible: at this moment there are some 300 formal requests awaiting decision, a process which could take forever. There is always a journalist waiting in a Havana hotel, after having appealed to all kinds of sponsors to see him. Some wait for months. They get indignant about not knowing who to turn to, because no one knows for sure what the right steps are for getting to him. The truth is that there are none. It is not unusual for some lucky journalist to ask him a casual question in the course of a public appearance and for the dialogue to end in an interview several hours' long on every conceivable subject. He takes a long time over each question, venturing out on the least-expected, difficult terrain without ever being carelessly imprecise, knowing that a single ill-used word can cause irreparable damage. In these rare formal interviews he tends to grant the time requested, however his unpredictable elasticity often prolongs the time, once stimulated by the dynamics of the dialogue. Only in very special cases does he ask to see the questions beforehand. He has never refused to answer any question, provocative though it may be, nor has he ever lost his patience. Sometimes the two hours planned turn into four, and nearly always into six. Or 17, as was the case in the interview with Gianni Minà[2] for Italian television, and which is one of the longest he has granted, and also

---

[2] This interview was published by Ocean Press, *An Encounter with Fidel* (1991)

one of the most complete.

Ultimately very few interviews please him, least of all the written transcripts, which in the interests of space tend to sacrifice the exactitude and the nuances particular to his personal style. He thinks that the television interviews end up unnatural because of the inevitable fragmentation, and it seems to him unjust to have given up to five hours of his life for a seven-minute program. But what is most regrettable, for both Fidel Castro and his listeners, is that even the best journalists, especially the Europeans, do not have even the curiosity to square their questions with reality. They aspire to the trophy with questions written according to the political obsessions and cultural prejudices of their own countries, without taking the trouble to find out for themselves what today's Cuba is really like, what the dreams and real frustrations of its people are: the truth of their lives. In this way they deprive the Cuban person in the street of an opportunity to talk to the world, and they deny themselves the professional achievement of questioning Fidel Castro, not about European suppositions, which are so distant, but about the anxieties of his own people, and especially in this time of great decisions.

In conclusion, listening to Fidel Castro in so many and diverse circumstances, I have asked myself many times if his zeal for conversation does not obey an organic need to hold at all costs to the guiding thread of truth amid the hallucinatory mirages of power. I have asked myself this over the course of many dialogues, public and private. But above all in the most difficult and fruitless, with those who in his presence lose their naturalness and aplomb and speak to him in theoretical formulas that have nothing to do with reality. Or with those who whisk the truth out of his sight so as not to give him more reasons for concern than he already has. He knows it. To one official who did that to him he said: "You hide truths from me so as not to trouble me, but when at last I discover them I will die from the effects of facing so many truths that you will have failed to tell me." The most serious, however, are the truths they hide from him to conceal shortcomings, because beside the enormous achievements which sustain the revolution — the political, scientific, sports, cultural achievements — there is a colossal bureaucratic incompetence affecting nearly every order of daily life, and most particularly domestic happiness. This has obliged Fidel Castro himself, nearly 30 years after victory, to personally deal with such extraordinary matters as the making of bread and the distribution of beer.

Everything is different, on the other hand, when he talks to the people in the street. The conversation then recovers the expressiveness and crude frankness of real affection. Of his various civilian and military names, only one is left to him: Fidel. They surround him without risks, they use the familiar *tú* (you) form of address with him, they argue with him, they contradict him, they make demands of him, with a channel of immediate transmission through which the truth flows in torrents. It is then, rather than in privacy, that the rare human being shielded from sight by the brilliance of his own image is discovered. This is the Fidel Castro I believe I know, after innumerable hours of conversation, through which the phantom of politics does not often pass. A man of austere ways and insatiable illusions, with an old-fashioned formal education, of cautious words and simple manners, and incapable of conceiving any idea which is not out of the ordinary. He dreams that his scientists will find the cure for cancer, and has created a world power foreign policy on an island without fresh water, 84 times smaller than its main enemy. Such is the discretion with which he protects his privacy that his intimate life has ended up being the most impenetrable enigma of his legend. He has the nearly mystical conviction that the greatest achievement of the human being is the proper formation of conscience and that moral incentives, rather than material ones, are capable of changing the world and moving history forward. I believe he is one of the greatest idealists of our time, and perhaps this may be his greatest virtue, although it has also been his greatest danger.

Many times I have seen him arrive at my house very late at night, still trailing the last scraps of a limitless day. Many times I have asked him how things were going, and more than once he answered me: "Very well, we have all the reservoirs full." I have seen him open the refrigerator to eat a piece of cheese, which was perhaps the first thing he had eaten since breakfast. I have seen him telephone a friend in Mexico to ask her for the recipe for a dish he had liked, and I have seen him copy it down leaning against the counter, among the still unwashed pots and pans from dinner, while someone on television sang an ancient song: "Life is an Express Train That Travels Thousands of Leagues." I have heard him in his few moments of nostalgia evoking the pastoral dawns of his rural childhood, the sweetheart of his youth who left, the things he could have done differently to win from life. One night, while he was eating vanilla ice-cream in slow little spoonfuls, I saw him so overwhelmed by the weight of the destinies of so many people, so removed from himself, that for an instant he seemed different to me from the man he had always been. Then I asked him what he would most like to do in this world, and he answered immediately: "Just hang around on some street corner."

໖

1

Childhood and Youth

I could say, first, that I come from a religious nation and, second, that I come from a religious family. At least, my mother was a very religious woman, a deeply religious woman and more religious than my father was.

Betto: Was your mother from the countryside?

Castro: Yes.

Betto: Cuban?

Castro: Yes, from a farm family.

Betto: And your father?

Castro: My father, too, came from a farm family. He was a very poor farmer from Galicia, Spain. However, I would not say that my mother was religious because she had received any religious training.

Betto: Did she have faith?

Castro: There's no doubt that she had a great deal of faith, and I would like to add that she learned how to read and write when she was practically an adult.

Betto: What was her name?

Castro: Lina.

Betto: And your father's?

Castro: Angel. My mother was practically illiterate. She learned how to read and write all by herself. I don't remember her ever having a teacher other than herself. She never mentioned one. With

This is a slightly abridged excerpt from a 24-hour interview with Fidel Castro by Brazilian liberation theologist, Frei Betto, in May 1985 published as Fidel and Religion *by Ocean Press.*

great effort she tried to learn. I never heard of her ever having gone to school. She was self-taught. She could not attend school or church or receive religious training. I think her religious beliefs had their origin in some family tradition, for her parents — especially her mother, my grandmother — were also very religious.

Betto: Was this religiousness limited to the home, or did she attend church frequently?

Castro: Well, it could not involve frequent church attendance, because there was no church where I was born, far from any city.

Betto: Where were you born?

Castro: In the north-central part of what used to be Oriente Province, near Nipe Bay.

Betto: What was the name of the town?

Castro: Well, it wasn't a town. There was no church; it wasn't a town. It was a farm called Birán. It had a few buildings. There was the family house and an annex containing a few small offices had been built on at one corner. Its architecture could be described as Spanish. You may wonder why a house built in Cuba should have Spanish architecture. It was because my father was a Spaniard from Galicia. In the villages there they had the custom of working a plot of land and keeping their animals under the house during the winter or throughout the year. They raised pigs and kept some cows there. That's why I said my house was based on Galician architecture, because it was built on stilts.

Interestingly, many years later the blueprints that were prepared in Cuba for the junior high schools in the countryside — very modern, solid buildings — called for piles, but not for the same reason. The idea was to eliminate the need for earthmoving operations to level the ground. Using a series of support columns in areas where the land sloped saved on such operations. Cement piles of different lengths were used to achieve a level base.

I've often wondered why my house had such tall stilts. Some of them were more than six feet high. The land under the house was uneven, so that, at the far end of the house, where the kitchen was located in an extension attached to the house, the stilts were shorter. At the other end there was a slight slope, and they were taller; but as I have already explained, this wasn't because of a desire to economize on earthmoving. Even though as a child I never stopped to think about such things, I'm convinced it was because of the Galician custom. Why? Because I remember that when I was very young — about three, four, five, or maybe six years old — the cows used to sleep under the house. There were 20 to 30 of them, and they were rounded up at dusk and driven to the house, where they slept below. They were milked there, and some were tied to the stilts.

I forgot to tell you that the house was made of wood. No mortar, cement or bricks. Plain wood. The stilts were made of hardwood, and they served as the foundation for the floor. The first story of the house, which I imagine was originally a square, was later extended with the addition of a hallway leading from one side of the house to several small rooms. The first room had cabinets where medicines were kept; it was called the medicine room. The next one was the bathroom. Then came a small pantry followed by a hallway which led to the dining room and finally the kitchen. Between the dining room and the kitchen, there was a flight of stairs leading down to the ground. Another addition was made later on. A sort of office was built onto one corner. By the time I began to notice things around me, the kitchen had already been built. Above the square portion, there was another floor called the lookout, where my parents and their first three children slept until I was four or five years old.

My father built the house in keeping with the customs of his native region. He also had a farm background and had no opportunity to study. So like my mother, he learned how to read and write all by himself, through sheer determination.

My father was the son of a very poor farmer in Galicia. At the time of Cuba's last War of Independence, which began in 1895, he was sent here as a Spanish soldier to fight. So here my father was, very young and drafted into military service as a soldier in the Spanish army. When the war was over, he was shipped back to Spain, but it seems he had taken a liking to Cuba. Along with many other immigrants, he left for Cuba in the early years of this century. Penniless and with no relatives here, he got himself a job.

Important investments were made in that period. U.S. citizens had seized the best land in Cuba and had started to destroy forests, build sugar mills and grow sugarcane, all of which involved big investments in those days. My father worked in one of the sugar mills.

The last War of Independence began in 1895 and ended in 1898. Spain had been virtually defeated when the United States staged its opportunistic intervention in that war. It sent soldiers; took over

Puerto Rico, the Philippines, and some other islands in the Pacific; and occupied Cuba. It could not seize Cuba permanently, because Cuba had been fighting for a long time. Even though their numbers were small, the Cuban people had been fighting heroically for many years. The United States did not plan to seize Cuba openly, because the cause of Cuba's independence had extensive support in Latin America and the world as a whole. As I have often said, Cuba was the 19th century's Vietnam.

My father returned to Cuba and began working. Later, he apparently got a group of workers together. He managed them and contracted the men to work for a U.S. firm. He set up a sort of small enterprise that, as far as I can remember, cleared land to plant sugarcane or felled trees to supply sugar mills with firewood. It's possible that, as the organizer of that enterprise with a group of men under him, he began to make a profit. In other words, my father was clearly a very active, enterprising person, and he had an instinctive sense of organization.

I don't know very much about the early years, because when I had a chance to inquire, I wasn't as curious as I am now. And now, who is able to tell us about his experiences?

I can't really remember many indications that my father was a religious person. I could not even say whether or not he really had any religious faith, but I do remember that my mother was very religious, just like my grandmother.

Betto: How was Christmas celebrated in your house?

Castro: In the traditional way. Christmas Eve was a time for celebration. Then came New Year's Eve, which involved a party that would go on till past midnight. I think there was also a religious holiday on the day of *Santos Inocentes* [Holy Innocents' Day], which I think was celebrated on December 28. The custom was to play tricks on people, to pull their leg or tell them some tall tale and say, "Fooled you, didn't I?" That was also part of the Christmas season.

Betto: When did your father die?

Castro: He died in 1956 before I came back from Mexico on the *Granma* expedition.[1]

My father died on October 21, 1956, two months after my 30th

---

[1] In December 1956, Fidel Castro and 81 others sailed a small yacht, *Granma*, from Mexico to launch the guerrilla struggle that culminated in the overthrow of the Batista dictatorship.

birthday. In December 1956 when I came back from Mexico with my small expedition, I was 30. I was 26 when we attacked the Moncada garrison,[2] and I spent my 27th birthday in prison.

Betto: And your mother; when did she die?

Castro: On August 6, 1963, three and a half years after the triumph of the revolution.

Rural life

We were talking about the countryside, where we lived, what the house was like, what my parents were like, and the educational level they had achieved in spite of their very poor background. I have mentioned the house and how it had incorporated Spanish traditions.

There was no town — only a few buildings — where we lived. When I was a child the cows were kept under the house. Later, they were moved somewhere else. In addition, there was always a small pen with pigs and poultry under the house, just like in Galicia. The place was inhabited by hens, ducks, guinea fowl, turkeys, some geese and pigs — all kinds of domestic animals. Later, a barn was built around 30 or 40 meters away from the house. A small slaughterhouse was close by, and there was a small smithy, where tools, plows and other farm implements were repaired, in front of the barn. The bakery was around 30 or 40 meters away from the house in a different direction. The elementary school — a small public school — was around 60 meters from the house on the other side of the bakery, next to the main road. That dirt road, which was called a highway, ran south from the municipal capital. The general store — the commercial center — was also owned by my family and had a leafy tree in front. The post office and telegraph office were opposite the store. Those were the main facilities there.

Betto: Your family owned the store?

Castro: Yes, but not the post office or the little schoolhouse. They were public property. All the rest belonged to my family. By the time I was born my father had already accumulated some resources, a certain degree of wealth.

Betto: When were you born?

Castro: On August 13, 1926. If you want to know the time, I think it was around 2:00 in the morning. Maybe that had something to do with my guerrilla spirit, with my revolutionary activities. Nature and

---

[2] July 26, 1953.

the time of my birth must have had some influence. There are other factors that should be taken into account now, right? What kind of a day it was and whether or not nature has anything to do with the lives of people. Anyway, I think I was born early in the morning. Therefore, I was born a guerrilla, because I was born at around 2:00 in the morning.

Betto: Yes, part of a conspiracy.

Castro: A bit of a conspiracy.

Betto: At least, the number 26 seems to have had quite a bearing on your life.

Castro: Well, I was born in 1926; that's true. I was 26 when I began the armed struggle, and I was born on the 13th, which is half of 26. Batista staged his coup d'état in 1952, which is twice 26. Now that I think of it, there may be something mystical about the number 26.

Betto: You were 26 when you began the struggle. The attack on the Moncada was on the 26th of July, and it gave rise to the July 26th Movement.

Castro: And we landed in 1956, which is the round number of 30 plus 26.

I've been describing what we had on the farm, but there's something else. The pit for cockfights was around 100 meters from the house, on the main road. During the sugar harvest, cockfights were held there every Sunday — cockfights, not bullfights — also on December 25, around New Year's and every holiday. The cockfighting fans would gather there, and some of them brought their own fighting cocks. Others limited themselves to betting. Many poor people lost their small incomes there. When they lost, they went home broke; when they won, they immediately spent the money on rum and parties.

Not far from the pit there were some poor dwellings, huts made of palm thatch with dirt floors. Most of them were inhabited by Haitian immigrants who worked on the farms, planting and cutting sugarcane. They had come to Cuba early in the 20th century and led a miserable existence. Even way back then there were Haitian immigrants in Cuba. It seems the work force in Cuba was not large enough, which is why Haitian immigrants came. The huts where the workers and their families lived were scattered along the main road and other roads, including the one that led to the railway that was used to transport the sugarcane. They also lived beside the rail tracks.

The farm's main crop was sugarcane. Cattle was next and, after that, horticulture. There were bananas, root vegetables, small plots planted to cereals, some vegetables, coconut trees and various fruit trees; there was a 10- to 12-hectare citrus grove near the house. The cane fields were farther away, closer to the railroad line that was used to take the sugarcane to the sugar mill.

By the time I started to take note of my surroundings, my family owned some land and leased some more. How much land did my father own? I'll tell you in hectares, even though we measure land in *caballerías* in Cuba. One *caballería* is equal to 13.4 hectares. My father owned around 800 hectares of land. A hectare is a square, each side of which is 100 meters long — that is, 10,000 square meters. Apart from that, my father leased some land. It was not as good as the land he owned, but it covered a much larger area, around 10,000 hectares.

Well, he had leased all that land. Most of it was hilly, with steep slopes, large areas densely wooded with pine trees, and a plateau at an altitude of 700–800 meters. Up there the soil is red, and there are large deposits of nickel and other metals. Since 1959, the area has been reforested. I liked that plateau very much, because it was cool. When I was around 11 years old, I used to go there on horseback. The horses had to struggle, climbing up the steep hillsides, but once they got there they would stop sweating and would be dry in a matter of minutes. It was marvelously cool up there because a breeze was always blowing through the tall, dense pine trees, whose tops met, forming a kind of roof. The water in the many brooks was ice-cold, pure and delicious. That whole area was leased; it did not belong to the family.

Several years later the family's income grew with a new asset: lumber. Some of the land that my father had leased included forested areas, which were exploited for the lumber. Other sections consisted of hills where cattle were raised, and another part was used for growing sugarcane and other crops.

Betto: So your father rose from being a poor farmer to a landowner.

Castro: I have a photo of the house in Galicia where my father was born. It was very small, about the size of this room — from 10 to 12 meters long and from six to eight meters wide. It was made of stone, which was abundant in the area and was often used by the farmers for the construction of their rustic dwellings. That was the house where the family lived. A one-room house, combination bedroom and kitchen. I imagine there were animals too. The family did not own even a square meter of land.

In Cuba he bought around 800 hectares of land and leased some more from some veterans of the War of Independence. It would take a good deal of research to find out how those veterans of the War of Independence came to own 10,000 hectares of land. Of course, those two veterans had been high-ranking officers in the War of Independence. I never thought about doing any research on the matter, but I imagine it was easy for them to get it. There was plenty of land at the time, and in one way or another they managed to buy it, perhaps by paying a very low price. People from the United States bought extensive tracts of land at very low prices, but I can't imagine what money or other resources those veterans had that enabled them to buy the land. Afterward, they got a percentage from the sale of the sugarcane that was grown there, plus a percentage from the sale of the lumber that was taken from their forests. They had independent means, lived in Havana, and had other businesses on the side. I can't really say whether those people got title to that land legally or illegally.

That vast extent of land was of two types: the land that my father owned and the land that he leased.

How many people lived on that vast latifundium at that time? Hundreds of workers' families, many of them worked small plots that my father let them have so they could grow crops for their own consumption. There were also some farmers who grew sugarcane, who were known as *subcolonos*. Their situation was not as difficult as that of the workers. How many families were there in all? Two hundred, maybe 300; when I was around 11 years old, around 1,000 people lived in that vast area.

This should give you an idea of the environment in which I was born and raised. There was not a single church, not even a small chapel.

Betto: Nor did a priest ever visit the place.

Castro: No, a priest used to show up once a year for baptisms. The area where I lived belonged to a municipality called Mayarí, and a priest used to come from the municipal seat, 36 kilometers away by the highway.

Betto: Were you baptized there?

Castro: No; I was baptized in Santiago de Cuba, several years after I was born.

Betto: How old were you then?

Castro: I think I was around five or six. I was one of the last children in my family to be baptized.

Religious influences

Let me explain something: in that place there was no church, no priests, and no religious training whatsoever. You asked me if those hundreds of families were believers. I would say that generally speaking they were. As a rule, everybody there had been baptized. I remember that those who hadn't been baptized were called "Jews." I could not understand what the term Jew meant. (I'm referring to the time when I was four or five years old.) I knew the word meant a very noisy, dark-colored bird, and every time somebody said "he's a Jew," I thought they were talking about that bird. Those were my first impressions. Anyone who hadn't been baptized was a "Jew."

There was no religious training. The school was a small, non-denominational school. About 15 to 20 children went there. I was sent there because there was no nursery school. I was the third oldest child in my family, and my nursery school was that school. They sent me there when I was very young. They had nothing else to do with me, so they sent me there with my older sister and brother.

I can't remember when I learned how to read and write. All I remember is that they used to put me in a small desk in the front row, where I could see the blackboard and listen to everything that was being said. I think it was there that I learned reading, writing and arithmetic. How old was I then? Probably four, or maybe five.

Religion was not taught in that school. You were taught the national anthem and told about the flag, the coat of arms and things like that. It was a public school.

Those families had different beliefs. I remember what people in the countryside thought about religion. They believed in God and also in a number of saints. Some of those saints were in the Liturgy — they were official saints. Others weren't. Everybody had their own saint, after whom they were named. You were told that your saint's day was very important, and you were very happy when it came around. April 24 was my saint's day, because there's a saint called Fidel. There was another saint before me, I want you to know!

Betto: I thought the name Fidel came from "he who has faith," which can also refer to fidelity.

Castro: In that case, I'm completely in agreement with my name in terms of fidelity and faith. Some have religious faith, and others have another kind. I've always been a man of faith, confidence and optimism.

Betto: If you didn't have faith, the revolution might not have triumphed in this country.

Castro: Yet, when I tell you why I'm called Fidel, you'll laugh. You see, the origin of the name isn't so idyllic. I had no name of my own. I was called Fidel because of somebody who was going to be my godfather. But before we take up baptism once more, let me finish my description of the environment.

At that time those farmers had all kinds of beliefs. They believed in God, in the saints, and in saints who weren't in the Liturgy.

Betto: They believed in the Virgin.

Castro: Of course, that was a widespread belief. They believed in Our Lady of Charity, Cuba's patron saint. They were all fervent believers in her. They all believed in several saints who weren't in the Liturgy, including St. Lazarus the Leper. It was practically impossible to find anyone who did not believe in St. Lazarus. Many people also believed in spirits and ghosts. I remember that, as a child, I heard stories about spirits, ghosts and apparitions. People believed in superstitions, too: for example, if a rooster crowed three times without getting an answer, that meant some tragedy might occur. If an owl flew over at night and you could hear the sound of its wings and its screech — I think they called it "the owl's song" — that, too, was a harbinger of tragedy. If a saltshaker fell to the floor and broke into pieces, the only way to forestall tragedy was to pick up some of the salt and throw it over your left shoulder. There were all kinds of very superstitions. In that sense, the world I was born into was quite primitive with all kinds of beliefs and superstitions: spirits, ghosts and animals that were harbingers of doom. That's the environment I remember.

This environment was reflected in my own family, to some extent. That's why I would say they were very religious people. My mother was a Catholic Christian, and her beliefs and faith were closely associated with the Catholic Church.

Betto: Did your mother teach her children to pray?

Castro: Well, not exactly. She did the praying. I could not say that she taught me, because I was sent to a school in Santiago de Cuba when I was about four-and-a-half years old, but I heard her when she prayed.

Betto: Did she say the rosary?

Castro: The rosary, Hail Mary and the Our Father.

Betto: Did she have any statues of Our Lady of Charity?

Castro: There were many statues of saints: Our Lady of Charity, the patron saint of Cuba; St. Joseph; Christ; and other Madonnas. There were many statues of saints recognized by the Catholic Church. There was also one of St. Lazarus, who was not one of the official saints of the Catholic Church.

My mother was a fervent believer; she prayed every day. She always lighted candles to the Virgin and the saints. She requested things from them and prayed to them in many circumstances. She made vows on behalf of any family member who became ill or who was in a difficult situation. And she not only made the vows but kept them, as well. One of those vows might be to visit the sanctuary and light a candle there or to help somebody out; this happened very frequently.

My aunts and my grandmother were also very firm believers. My grandmother and my grandfather — my maternal grandparents — lived about a kilometer away from our home at that time.

I remember when an aunt of mine died in childbirth. I remember her burial. If I could determine the exact date, I could tell you when I had my first image of death. I know there was great sadness, a lot of crying. I even remember that, a small boy at the time, I was taken to the home of an aunt who had married a Spaniard and lived a kilometer away from my home.

Betto: Did both the mother and the baby die, or was it only the mother?

Castro: The mother died, and the daughter — it was a girl — was raised with us. That is the first memory of death I have: that of my aunt.

My maternal grandparents were also very poor; they came from a very poor family. My grandfather hauled sugarcane in an ox cart. He, like my mother, was born in the western part of the country, in Pinar del Río Province. During the early years of the century he and the rest of the family moved to what used to be called Oriente Province, 1,000 kilometers away from his home, in an ox cart, and settled there.

My grandfather and his whole family moved: my mother and my uncles and aunts. Two of my mother's brothers also worked there as ox-cart drivers.

My grandmother was very religious. I would say that my mother's and my grandmother's religious beliefs were the result of family tradition. Both of them were very fervent believers.

I remember that after the triumph of the revolution in 1959, I went to visit them, here in Havana. They were together, and my grandmother had some health problems. The room was full of saints and prayer cards. Throughout the struggle, which entailed great risks, both my mother and my grandmother made all kinds of vows on behalf of our lives and safety. The fact that we came out of the struggle alive must have greatly increased their faith. I was very respectful of their beliefs. They told me about the vows they had made and their deep faith. This was after the revolution had triumphed in 1959. I always listened to them with great interest and respect. Even though I did not share their view of the world, I never argued with them about these things, because I could see the strength, courage and comfort they got from their religious feelings and beliefs. Of course, their feelings were neither rigid nor orthodox but something very much their own and very strongly felt. It was a part of the family tradition.

I think my father was more concerned about other matters — political issues, everyday struggles, the organization of tasks and activities. His comments referred mainly to other kinds of problems. Rarely, if ever, did I hear him make any religious comments. Maybe he was a skeptic in terms of religion. That was my father.

In that sense it may be said that I came from a Christian family, especially as regards my mother and my grandmother. I think that my grandparents in Spain were also very religious, though I never met them. I was aware of the religious feeling of my mother and her family.

Why I was named Fidel

The reason why they called me Fidel is interesting. Baptisms were very important ceremonies in the countryside among all the farmers — even among those who had no religious background. Baptisms were a very popular institution. Since the risk of death was much greater and life expectancy in the countryside was low in those days, farm families believed that the godfather was the child's second father. He was supposed to help him. If the father died, his child would still have somebody who would help and support him. That was a deep-rooted feeling. They sought out their most trusted friends; sometimes the godfather was an uncle. I would have to ask my older sister and Ramón, who was the second oldest, who their godfathers were, but I think they were uncles.

We were the children of a second marriage. There were children from the first marriage, and I remember that we knew them. I was the third child of the second marriage, from which there were seven children in all: four daughters and three sons.

I had been chosen to become the godson of a friend of my father's. He was a very wealthy man who had some business dealings with my father. He sometimes lent my father money for the house and other expenses at a set rate of interest; he was something like the family banker. He was very rich, much richer than my father. People said he was a millionaire, and nobody ever said that about my father. To be a millionaire in those days meant lots and lots of money, when people used to earn a dollar or a peso a day. At that time my father's property could not be assessed at such a high price. Even though he was well-off, my father wasn't a millionaire.

So that man was chosen to be my godfather; but he was very busy and lived in Santiago de Cuba. He had business interests throughout the province. Apparently circumstances did not favor simultaneous visits to Birán by that wealthy man, my godfather, and a priest. While awaiting this coincidence, I remained unbaptized, and I remember that people called me a "Jew." I was four or five and was already being criticized. I did not know the meaning of the word "Jew," but there was no doubt that it had a negative connotation, that it was something disgraceful. It was all because I hadn't been baptized, but I wasn't really to blame for that.

Before being baptized, I was sent to Santiago de Cuba. My teacher had led my family to believe that I was a very industrious student. She made them believe that I was smart and had a talent for learning. That was the real reason why they sent me to Santiago de Cuba when I was around five; I was taken from a world in which I lived with no material problems and sent to a city where I lived in poverty and was hungry.

Betto: When you were five.

Castro: Yes, when I was five and had had no previous knowledge of hunger.

Betto: Why were you poor?

Castro: I was poor because the teacher's family was poor. She was the only one earning any money. That was during the economic crisis of the 1930s, around 1931 or 1932. The family consisted of two sisters and their father, and one of the sisters was the only one who had a job. Sometimes she would not be paid or would be paid only after a long wait. During the great economic crisis of the early 1930s, salaries often weren't paid and the people were very poor.

I went to Santiago de Cuba to live in a very small frame house that leaked like a sieve when it rained. The house is still there. During the school year, the teacher kept working in Birán and her sister had to live on that salary. My family sent 40 pesos for my board, an amount that had the same purchasing power as 300 or 400 pesos now. There were two of us, my older sister and me. In view of that poverty, their not receiving salaries, and the fact that they wanted to save, not much money went for food. There were five people to be fed — later six, when my brother Ramón came a few months later. We got a small container with a little rice, some beans, sweet potatoes, plantains and things like that. The container arrived at noon, and it was shared first by five and then by six people, for lunch and dinner. I used to think I had a huge appetite; the food always seemed delicious. Actually, it was just that I was always hungry. It was a rough period.

Later the teacher's sister married the Haitian consul in Santiago de Cuba. Since my wealthy godfather hadn't materialized and the baptism hadn't been performed — I was then around five years old — a solution had to be found. I guess the fact that I was called a "Jew" is also linked to some religious prejudices that we can discuss later on. Anyway, finally I was baptized, and the Haitian consul became my godfather, because he had married the teacher's sister, Belén, who was a good and noble person. She was a piano teacher, but she had no work or students.

Betto: So your godfather wasn't your father's wealthy friend after all.

Castro: No, it wasn't the rich man; it was the consul in Santiago de Cuba of the poorest country in Latin America. The teacher was a mestizo, as was my godmother.

Betto: Are they still living?

Castro: No, they died a long time ago. I don't feel any resentment toward them, even though the teacher was doing it to make a profit from the 40 pesos for each of us my family paid every month. But that was a difficult period in my life.

One afternoon they took me to the cathedral in Santiago de Cuba. I don't remember the exact date. I may have been six when I was finally baptized, because I had already been there for a while and had had some hard times before the day they took me to the cathedral. They sprinkled me with holy water and baptized me and I became a regular citizen, the same as the rest. At long last I had been baptized. I had a godfather and a godmother, even though the former wasn't the millionaire my parents had originally chosen, Don Fidel Pino Santos. By the way, a nephew of his is a very valuable comrade of ours working for the revolution: an outstanding economist, a hard worker, a very able comrade — an economist and a communist. He's been a communist ever since his youth, even though he was the nephew of that very wealthy man who bequeathed me his name.

So you can see how, by pure chance, you can receive a fitting name. That was the only fitting thing I received during that whole period.

Betto: What was the consul's name?

Castro: Luis Hibbert.

Betto: Today your name could be Luis Castro.

Castro: My name could be Luis Castro if they had asked the consul to be my godfather from the beginning. Well, there have been some very prestigious Luises in the history of humanity — kings and saints. By any chance, hasn't there been a pope named Luis?

Betto: I don't remember. I am not well versed in the history of the popes. But I have a brother whose name is Luis.

Castro: They could wait six years to baptize me, but they could not wait six years to give me a name. So that is the origin of my name, which I actually owe to a very rich man — although not exactly the rich epicurean of the Bible. To tell you the truth, it is sad to talk about people who died a long time ago, but my potential godfather had the reputation of being a very frugal man, excessively frugal. I don't think that he had anything in common with his biblical predecessor.

He didn't give me many gifts, none that I can remember. He did make loans to my father, with the corresponding interest, which at that time was under what it is now — maybe about 6 percent.

Later, that man became a politician and even ran for representative. Of course, now you are going to ask for what party. Well, for the government's party, because he always was with the government's party. Do you understand? But later, his son became a representative from the opposition party, so everything was settled.

When the election campaign started, I remember that my father supported him. You can see the lessons in democracy I received at an early age. A lot of money circulated in my house at election time. To put it more accurately, my father spent a lot of money to help his friend in each election. In other words, my father spent a lot of his money to help his candidate. That's what politics was like then.

Of course, as a landowner, my father controlled most of the votes, because many people didn't know how to read and write. To be given a job in the rural areas was considered a big favor then, as was being allowed to live on somebody else's land. Therefore, the farmer or worker who received such a favor — and all the rest of his family — had to be grateful to his patron and vote for his candidate. In addition, there were ward heelers. Who were they? Experts in politics. This did not mean that they were advisers well versed in sociology, law or economics; rather, they were smart farmers in each area who obtained a specific government job or who were given money during the election campaigns to get votes for a councilman, a mayor, a provincial governor, a representative, a senator, or even the president. There were no TV or radio campaigns then; I think they would have cost even more.

This was when I was about 10. I knew a lot about politics by the time I was 10, because I had seen so many things!

I remember that when I was home on vacation during one election period, the safe that was kept in the room where I slept became a problem. You know that children like to sleep late, but I could not because there was a lot of coming and going very early in the morning — around 5:30 — during the election campaign. The safe was constantly being opened and closed, making an inevitable metallic bang. The ward heelers would arrive, and they had to be given money. This was all done in the most altruistic spirit, because my father did it out of friendship. I don't remember a single instance, apart from the loans, when that man solved any of my father's problems or gave him funds for political campaigns. My father undertook those expenses on his own. That's what politics was like, and that's what I learned as a child.

There were a number of people who controlled a certain number of votes, especially in the more remote areas, because the people who lived closer in were controlled directly by the most trusted employees on the farm. But ward heelers who controlled 80 to 100 votes would come from 30 to 40 kilometers away. Afterward, those votes had to appear in the corresponding electoral college or the ward heeler lost his prestige, award or job. That's what election campaigns were like in the rural areas.

The man who was supposed to become my godfather became a representative. My real godfather, the poor one, the Haitian consul, had some difficulties by then. In 1933, the Machado dictatorship[3] was overthrown by a revolution — I was seven in 1933 — and at the beginning that revolution passed some laws of a nationalist nature. At the time many people were unemployed and were starving, while, for example, many stores in Havana that were owned by Spaniards would employ only Spaniards. There was a nationalist demand that a percentage of the jobs be given to Cubans. It may have been a fair demand in principle, but in practice it gave rise to some cruel measures in certain circumstances, taking jobs away from people who, though they were foreigners, were very poor and had no other way to earn a living.

I still remember with genuine sorrow how, for example, in Santiago de Cuba and the rest of Oriente Province, they started to expel the Haitian immigrants who had lived in Cuba for many years. Those Haitians had left their country years before, fleeing from starvation. They grew and cut sugarcane, making great sacrifices, tremendous sacrifices. Their wages were so low they were almost slaves. I'm absolutely sure that 19th century slaves had a higher standard of living and better care than those Haitians.

Slaves were treated like animals, but they were given food and taken care of so they would live and produce. They were preserved as part of the plantations' capital; those tens of thousands of Haitian immigrants could eat only when they worked, and nobody cared if

[3] General Gerardo Machado Morales, president of Cuba 1925–33. He was known for his pro-U.S. stance and brutal suppression of opposition. He finally fled Cuba in 1933, a month before the "Sergeants' Revolt" led by Sergeant Fulgencio Batista on September 5, 1933.

they lived or died of starvation. They suffered from all kinds of deprivations.

The so-called 1933 revolution was, in fact, a movement against injustice and abuse. It called for the nationalization of the electric company and other foreign enterprises, and for the nationalization of employment. In the name of the nationalization of employment, tens of thousands of those Haitians were mercilessly deported to Haiti. According to our revolutionary ideas that was an inhuman thing to do. What happened to them? How many of them survived?

My godfather was still the consul in Santiago de Cuba at that time, and a big ship with two smokestacks, the *La Salle*, arrived in the city. I was taken to see it, because the arrival of a two-stack ship in Santiago de Cuba was a special event. The ship was full of Haitians who were being taken back to Haiti after being expelled from Cuba.

Later on, my godfather lost his job and his consulate, and I think he had no income — nothing — and he, too, returned to Haiti. My godmother remained alone for many years, and it was only after a long time that he returned to Cuba. I was already an adult by then. He went to Birán, where he sought refuge and lived for awhile. He had no way to earn a living.

Early schooling

During the period I told you about, I was sent to Santiago de Cuba while still very young. I had many unmet needs and went through a lot of hardship. Around a year later, things started to improve somewhat. At one point, my parents became aware of the difficulties I was facing. They protested and took me back to Birán. But after the teacher explained, there was a reconciliation and I was sent back to her house in Santiago de Cuba. The situation, of course, improved after the scandal. How much time did I spend there in all? At least two years.

In the beginning I was not sent to school; my godmother gave me classes. Those classes consisted of having me study the addition, subtraction, multiplication and division tables that were printed on the cover of my notebook. I learned them by heart and I learned them so well I've never forgotten them. Sometimes I calculate almost as quickly as a computer.

I had no textbook, only my notebook and some notes. I learned arithmetic, reading, writing and taking notes. My spelling and handwriting must have improved a little. I think I spent around two years there just wasting my time. The only useful aspect was the experience of tough, difficult conditions, hardships and sacrifices. I think I was the victim of exploitation, in view of the income that family got from my parents.

Since you mentioned religious beliefs, one of the first things we were taught to believe in was the Three Wise Men. I must have been three or four the first time the Wise Men came. I even remember the things they brought me: some apples, a toy car and some candy.

January 6 was the Epiphany. We were told that the Three Wise Men, who had traveled to pay homage to Christ when he was born, came every year to bring children presents.

I spent three Epiphanies with that family in Santiago. Therefore, I must have been there at least two and a half years.

Betto: So the capitalist Santa Claus never became popular in Cuba?

Castro: No, never. We had the Three Wise Men, who rode camels. Children wrote letters to the Three Wise Men: Caspar, Melchior and Balthazar. I can still remember the first letters I wrote when I was five and asked them for everything — cars, trains, movie cameras, the works. I would write long letters to the Three Wise Men on January 5. Then I looked for some grass, and I put it under my bed with some water. The disappointment came later.

Betto: What's that about the grass?

Castro: Since the Three Wise Men rode camels, you had to provide them with some grass and water, which you put under your bed.

Betto: All mixed up?

Castro: Either mixed up or the grass and water next to each other. You had to provide food and water for the camels, especially if you wanted the Three Wise Men to bring you lots of presents, everything you'd asked them for in your letter.

Betto: And what did the Three Wise Men eat?

Castro: Well, I don't know. Nobody remembered to leave food for the Three Wise Men. Maybe that's why they weren't very generous with me! The camels ate the grass and drank the water, but I got very few toys in exchange. I remember that my first present was a small cardboard trumpet; just the tip was made out of metal, something like aluminum. The trumpet was the size of a pencil.

For three consecutive years, I was given a trumpet; I should have become a musician! The second year's trumpet was half aluminum and half cardboard. The third time it was a trumpet with three small keys, made completely of aluminum.

I was attending school by then. When I finished my third year there, I was sent away to school, and then the changes began!

La Salle School

After being in Santiago de Cuba for about a year and a half or two years, I was sent to the La Salle School, which was six or seven blocks away. I went to school in the morning and went home for lunch. We had lunches then; we weren't hungry anymore. After lunch I went back to school. The Haitian consul, my godfather, was still with us when I enrolled in La Salle. It was a big step forward for me to go to school.

We were systematically taught the catechism, religion and some elements of biblical history. I must have been around six and a half or seven, but they kept me back in first grade. I had already learned to read and write, yet they had made me waste almost two years. I should have been in the third grade.

Once I started attending school my education was systematic; but the most important thing was the material and environmental improvement. For the first time I had teachers, classes, friends to play with, and many other activities that I had lacked when I was a single student studying arithmetic from the cover of a notebook. This lasted until I launched my first act of rebellion, when I was still very young.

Betto: What caused it?

Castro: I was tired of the whole situation. At the teacher's house, I was spanked every so often, and if I did not behave perfectly, they threatened to send me to boarding school. Then one day I realized that I would be better off in boarding school than in that house.

Betto: Who threatened you? Your brother and sister?

Castro: My godmother, my godfather, the teacher when she was on her vacation — everybody.

Betto: How did you rebel?

Castro: Those people had had a French education — I don't remember exactly how. They spoke perfect French. Maybe they had been to France or had attended a school in Haiti. They also had perfect manners, which they taught me when I was very young. Among other things, you weren't supposed to ask for anything. The very poor children used to have a penny to buy a *rayado* or *granizado*, which is what they called snow-cones, but I could not ask them for anything; that was forbidden, according to the rules of French education. If I asked another boy to give me some, the children, because of typical childish selfishness and the desperate poverty in which they lived used to say, "You're begging! I'm going to tell on you!" They knew the rules I had to follow.

That family had its code, and I'm not criticizing it. You were subjected to a lot of discipline. You had to speak in an educated way. You could not raise your voice. Naturally, you could not use improper language. When they threatened to send me to boarding school, I was already tired and had become aware of what had happened before, realizing that I had been starving and that I hadn't been treated fairly. I have not told you everything in full detail, because I don't want to make this an autobiography; I just want to touch on subjects that might be interesting.

So one day at school, I deliberately started to break all the rules and regulations. In what amounted to a conscious act of rebellion aimed at having them send me to boarding school, I raised my voice and said all the words I had been forbidden to use. That's the story of my first — though not my last — rebellion. I was in the first grade; I must have been seven at most.

Betto: So you were finally sent to boarding school?

Castro: Yes, and I began to be happy. For me, boarding school meant freedom.

Betto: How long were you at the La Salle boarding school?

Castro: Nearly four years. I was there from the second half of the first grade. Because of my good grades, I was promoted to the fifth grade straight from the third grade, so I made up for one of the years I had lost.

Betto: What was the religious training like? Was religion presented as something good and joyful, or was there a lot of talk about hell, punishment and God? What was it like? Was a lot of emphasis placed on going to mass, making sacrifices and doing penance, or were things more positive? How do you remember it?

Castro: I remember different periods, because I attended three different schools at various times in my life. It was really very hard for me to have any opinion on the matter during that first period.

First of all, I was away from my family. I had been sent to Santiago de Cuba, and this in itself caused some problems. I was away from my family, my home, the place I loved, where I used to play, run around and enjoy freedom. Then suddenly I was sent to a city where I had a difficult time, faced with material problems. I was far from my family, with people who weren't my relatives placed in charge of me. I was tired of the life in that house, that family, those rules. I had no religious problems; rather, I had material living problems and a personal situation that needed solving. Acting by instinct, or intuition, which was how I really functioned, I disobeyed that authority.

Then things changed. There was a distinct material improvement when I went to boarding school. After class, I could play in the schoolyard with all the other boys. I was no longer alone, and once or twice a week we were taken to the countryside and the ocean. We went to a small peninsula on the Bay of Santiago de Cuba, where there's an oil refinery and some other industrial projects now. The Christian Brothers rented a spot there near the beach. They had a resort and sports facilities. They would take us on Thursdays, because we did not have class on Thursday or Sunday. They divided the week into two parts: three days of classes, a break, and then two more days of classes. I was very happy at the boarding school, going to the beach every Thursday and Sunday and being free, fishing, swimming, hiking, taking part in sports. I was more interested in and concerned about those things.

The religious training, catechism, mass and other activities were normal parts of everyday life, just like classes and study periods. Then, as now, with too many meetings, what I liked most were the recesses. Religious training in those days was a natural thing; I could not make any value judgments at that time.

Betto: Talk of sin didn't make you afraid? Wasn't it stressed?

Castro: I did not become aware of those problems until later on, not during the first phase.

At that time, I studied religion just as I studied the history of Cuba. We accepted everything about the beginning of the world and everything in it as natural facts. They did not make us reason this out. I was more concerned about sports, the beach, nature and studying the different school subjects — that kind of thing. I did not really have any special religious inclination or vocation. That's a fact.

We usually had a vacation every three months, when we went home to the countryside. The countryside was freedom.

For example, Christmas Eve was wonderful, because it meant two weeks' vacation — and not just two weeks' vacation, but two weeks

of festivities and treats: cookies, candy and nougats. We had a lot of
them at my house. Many traditional Spanish products were always
bought for the Christmas season. When that time came, you were
always excited, from the time you took the train and then continued
on horseback until you finally arrived. In those days you had to take
a train and then a horse to get home. The roads were nothing but
huge mud holes. During the first few years in my house, there were
no cars or even electricity. We got electricity a little later. We would
use candles for light in the country.

Since we had experienced hunger and confinement in the city,
having that open space, guaranteed food and the festive atmosphere
around Christmas, Christmas Eve, New Year's Day and the
Epiphany was very attractive. We quickly learned that there were no
Three Wise Men, however. That was one of the first things that made
us skeptical. We began to discover that our parents were the ones who
brought the toys. The adults themselves robbed us of our innocence
too soon. It's not that I'm against the custom — I'm not making a
value judgment about that — but we quickly learned that some
trickery had been involved.

Christmas vacations were happy times. Holy Week was another
wonderful time, because we had another week of vacation at home.
Then there was summer vacation when we went swimming in the
rivers, running through the woods, hunting with slingshots and
riding horses. We lived in direct contact with nature and were quite
free during those times. That's what my childhood was like.

I had been born in the countryside and had lived there before the
problems arose that I've already told you about. When you enter the
third or fifth grade, you begin to learn a lot more and to observe
things.

Holy Week in the countryside meant days of great solemnity.
What was said? That Christ died on Good Friday. You could not talk
or joke or be happy, because Christ was dead and the Jews killed him
every year. This is another case in which accusations or popular
beliefs have caused tragedies and historical prejudices. I told you, I did
not know what that term meant; I first thought that those birds
called *judios* (Jews) had killed Christ.

You had to eat fish, no meat. Then came Holy Saturday, which
was a day of festivity, even though, as I understand it, the
Resurrection hadn't taken place yet. But the people used to say,

"Holy Saturday, day of celebration; Good Friday, day of silence and mourning." There in the countyside the stores were busy on Holy Saturday, and there were parties and cockfights that continued into Easter Sunday.

I would say that during that period I was more absorbed in the things I've mentioned; I wasn't in a position to evaluate the religious training then. But I did realize after a while that everything was taught like arithmetic: five times five is 25. That's how religion was taught.

Betto: Did the brothers seem more like teachers than religious workers, or did they also appear to be good religious workers?

Castro: Well, the Christian Brothers weren't really priests; they hadn't been trained for the priesthood. It was a much less demanding, less strict order than the Jesuits. I realized that later on when I went to the Jesuits' school.

Conflicts arose in the Christian Brothers' school. I had my second rebellion there. The education in that school was not bad, nor was the organization of the students' activities. There were around 30 boarding students, and we used to be taken out on Thursdays and Sundays for breaks, as I told you. The food was not bad. Life in general was not bad.

Those people hadn't had the training that the Jesuits had. Moreover, they used really reprehensible methods at times. Some teachers or school authorities hit the students every so often. My conflict there was over that, because of an incident with another student. It was a small quarrel typical of students of that age. I had the opportunity to see how violence is used against students in what would now be considered bad teaching methods. That was the first time the brother monitor in charge of the students hit me with a fair amount of violence. He slapped both sides of my face. It was a degrading and abusive thing. I was in the third grade, and I never forgot it. Later, when I was in the fifth grade, I was hit on the head twice. The last time I would not put up with it, and it ended in a violent personal confrontation between the monitor and me. After all that, I decided not to go back to that school.

I also saw some forms of favoritism toward some students at that institution. I also saw how money played a role. I was perfectly aware that some of the brothers displayed a great deal of interest in my family, giving us special treatment because we had a lot of land and were said to be rich. In other words, I saw clearly that material interest and deference related to money.

The teachers at La Salle were not as disciplined as the Jesuits. I would say they were less strict and less ethically solid than the Jesuits. I say this as a criticism, while also recognizing the positive things: the students' contact with the countryside, the scheduling of activities, a good education. But hitting students is monstrous and unacceptable. There was discipline; I'm not against the imposition of discipline. They had to discipline us. But you're older in the fifth grade; you have a sense of personal dignity; and violent methods, physical punishment, seems unthinkable to me.

Dolores College

Betto: Let's go on to the Jesuits. What was the school called?

Castro: It was the Dolores College (School of Our Lady of Sorrows) of Santiago de Cuba, a prestigious upper-class school.

Betto: When did you start boarding there?

Castro: At first, I went for a trial period, not as a boarder. I lived at the home of a businessman who was a friend of my father. I had to confront another new experience: changing schools. It was a much more rigorous school, and I found a lot of misunderstanding on the part of the adults who were caring for me. It was one of those families that takes in somebody else's child as a matter of friendship, rather than kindness. There were economic interests at play in those situations and, at any rate, a different relationship. I was not their son; they could not treat me like a son.

It is better to board at school, I'm convinced, than to be sent to the home of a friend, a family friend. Staying with family friends isn't advisable unless the people are kind — and such people do exist. The society in which I grew up was a society with many difficulties; the people had to make many sacrifices. On reflection, that society engendered tremendous selfishness, making people want to gain something out of every situation, rather than encouraging kindness and generosity.

Betto: And that society was considered Christian?

Castro: There are many people in the world today who call themselves Christians but do horrible things. Pinochet, Reagan and Botha, for example, consider themselves Christians.

The people I was living with practiced Christianity. That is, they went to mass. Could anything particularly bad be said about that family? No. Nor could I say that my godmother was a bad person, because she went hungry along with the rest of us. She did not have control in that house at the time. Her sister was in control as she received the salary, the income, and managed it. She was really a good, noble person. But this situation involved not a son — with whom another relationship generally exists — but rather a stranger who was there in that home.

I was in the fifth grade when I went to live with the businessman's family. I could not say they were bad people, but they weren't my family. They applied some strict, even arbitrary, rules. For example, they did not take into account the fact that I had had problems in my other school, as I've already explained, and that I had transferred to a more rigorous school. They did not consider the psychological factors involved in adapting to a new, more demanding school and new teachers. They wanted me to get the highest grades; they demanded it. If I did not get the highest grades, I didn't get that week's 10 cents for going to the movies, five cents for buying ice cream after the movies, and five cents on Thursday for buying some comic books. I remember this clearly. There were comic books for five cents that came from Argentina, a weekly called *El gorrión* [*The House Sparrow*]. I read some novels there, too. *De tal palo, tal astilla* [*Like Father, Like Son*] was one of them. The normal weekly allowance was 25 cents. If you did not get the highest grades, you didn't get the 25 cents. That measure was arbitrary and completely unfair, because they did not take my new circumstances into account. It was not the right psychological approach with an 11-year-old.

Why did they want me to get good grades? It was mainly a matter of pride and vanity, but other factors were involved too. It was a rather upper-class school. The people who had children in that school, boarding or otherwise, viewed it with vanity, as a form of social achievement. As a child, I suffered from many such things, for there was no one to guide me.

I began as a day student at the school, after Christmas vacation, after arguing a lot at home. I had to argue at home and demand that I be sent away to study. That's when I launched my battle to study. I had to struggle, because the people at my old school had told my parents that I had behaved badly, and those arbitrary reports had influenced my family. I said I would not accept not being allowed to study. I knew what the problem was. It stemmed from an abusive, violent act, the physical punishment of a student. I had very clear ideas about this matter — the result of instinct and some notions of justice and dignity that I was developing. When I was still quite young, I had begun to see some incorrect, unfair things by which I was victimized. I began to acquire values, of which I was very aware. I had to demand very firmly that I be sent away to study — perhaps not so much out of a love of study, but rather because I felt an injustice had been committed against me. My mother supported me; I convinced her first, and then she convinced my father. They sent me to Santiago de Cuba again, but as a day student. When I got there I began to have the problems I told you about.

Summer came and they left me in Santiago because my older sister was there studying. A black teacher from Santiago de Cuba came to tutor my sister. She was very well trained; her name was Professor Danger. She became interested in me. Since I had nothing else to do during my vacation, I did classes with my sister, who was preparing for high school. I answered all the questions in all the subjects the teacher taught, and this made her genuinely interested in me. I was not old enough to enter high school, so she began to draw up a study plan for both before and during the first year of high school at the same time. Then, when I was old enough, I could take the exams. She was the first person I ever met who encouraged me; who set a goal, an objective, for me and who motivated me. She got me interested in studying when I was young. I think you can stimulate children at that age with a specific objective. How old was I? Ten, or maybe 11.

Then a new phase began. When school began after that summer, I had to go to hospital to have my appendix out. I hadn't had anything more than mild discomfort, but in those days everybody had their appendix out. The wound got infected, and I spent three months in the hospital. The teacher's plan was forgotten, and I had to begin the sixth grade almost at the end of the first quarter.

After that I decided to board at the school. I was tired of that situation, so at the end of the first quarter, I suggested — or rather, firmly demanded — that I go as a boarder. I was already an expert in such disputes. I decided to create a situation in which they had no alternative but to send me to school as a boarder. Thus, between the first and sixth grades, I had to wage three battles to solve three problems.

By the time I started to board in the sixth grade, I was getting excellent grades, and in the seventh grade I was among the top students in my class. I also gained a lot in other ways, because of the world of sports and trips to the countryside I now enjoyed. I liked sports a lot — especially basketball, soccer and baseball.

I really liked soccer, but I liked basketball, too. I also played baseball and volleyball. I played everything. I always liked sports. For me sports were a diversion, and I put my energy into them.

I was in a school with more demanding, better-trained teachers with a much greater religious vocation. They were more devoted, able and disciplined than those at La Salle; they were incomparably better. I think it was good for me to go there. I met a different kind of person — teachers and other men who were interested in molding the students' character. They were Spaniards. In general, I think that the traditions of the Jesuits and their military spirit and organization go with the Spanish personality. They were very rigorous, demanding people, who were interested in their students, their character and behavior.

In other words, I acquired ethics and habits that weren't just religious. I was influenced by the teachers' authority and their moral values. They encouraged sports, hikes and trips to the mountains, which I loved. Sometimes I made the whole group wait two hours while I climbed a mountain, but they did not criticize me because I was making a great effort. They saw it as proof of an enterprising, tenacious spirit. Even if the activities were risky and difficult, they did not discourage them.

Betto: They never dreamed they were training a guerrilla.

Castro: Nor did I dream I was preparing to be a guerrilla, but every time I saw a mountain, the challenge of climbing it, of reaching the top, would seize me. How did they encourage me? I think they never put any obstacles in my way. Occasionally, the bus with the rest of the students would wait for me for two hours. At other times, when there were heavy downpours, I would swim across swollen rivers, not without risk. They always waited and never criticized me for this. In other words, if they noted characteristics in their students such as a spirit of adventure, sacrifice or effort, they encouraged them. They did not turn students into weaklings. The Jesuits were much more concerned about their students' character.

I disagree, however, with the prevailing political ideas they espoused. And I also do not agree with the way religion was taught.

Faith and convictions

From all this, you can draw some conclusions about how my character was shaped by the problems and difficulties I had to overcome and by my trials, conflicts and rebellions when I had no mentor or a guide to help me. I never really had a mentor. The person who came closest to being one was that black teacher from Santiago de Cuba. She set me a goal and inspired me; but everything fell apart when I got sick at the beginning of the school year and spent three months in the hospital.

As you can see, the misfortunes in my life did not create favorable conditions for a strong religious influence; instead they must have strongly influenced my political and revolutionary vocation.

Betto: What do you remember about the Jesuits' religious mission? Was it good, bad, tied to real life, or more oriented to heaven and the saving of souls? What was it like?

Castro: I can judge that better now. I also went to a Jesuit high school. Looking back on what influenced me, I think that in some ways it was not positive; everything was very dogmatic: "This is so because it has to be so." You had to believe it, even if you did not understand it. If you didn't, it was a fault, a sin, something worthy of punishment. I would say that reasoning played no role. Reasoning and feelings were not developed.

It seems to me that religious faith, like political belief, should be based on reasoning, on the development of thought and feelings. The two things are inseparable.

Betto: I don't want to get into a secular squabble between the Jesuits and the Dominicans, but the Dominicans are noted for placing greater value on the intelligence of faith, while the Jesuits place more emphasis on willpower.

Castro: I accept that some people may have a special leaning, a mystical spirit, a great religious vocation, a greater predisposition to religious faith, than other people. I could have been open to reason, and I think I was open to developing feelings. But it was not possible to inculcate a solid religious faith in me, because things were explained in an entirely dogmatic way.

If you have to accept things because you're told to, you can't argue or reason them out. Moreover, if the main motivation is reward or punishment — punishment more than reward — it is impossible to develop the reasoning and feelings that could be the basis of a sincere religious belief. That's what I think in retrospect.

The reward was very abstract. For a child, abstract rewards based on contemplation, on a state of happiness you had to imagine for all eternity, was more difficult to perceive than punishment. Punishment was easier to explain; a child is better prepared to understand punishment, everlasting hell and pain, suffering and eternal fire. Much more emphasis was placed on punishment and I really think this is a bad way to develop any kind of deep conviction in a human being. Later on, when I formed a belief and faith in the political arena, I firmly upheld specific values; I have never been able to imagine how a belief might be based on something that is not understood or inspired by fear or reward.

I believe that people's religious beliefs should be based on understandable reasons and the intrinsic value of their actions.

Betto: Unrelated to reward or punishment?

Castro: That's right. I think that what is done out of fear of punishment or in search of reward is not entirely altruistic or noble. It isn't really worthy of praise, admiration or esteem. In my revolutionary life and revolutionary concepts, when I've had to involve people in very difficult situations and very hard tests to be endured with total self-sacrifice and altruism, the most admirable thing was that they weren't motivated by the idea of reward or punishment. The Church has also gone through trials; it did so for many centuries. It suffered martyrdom and confronted it. I feel that this can only be explained by deep conviction.

I think conviction is what makes martyrs. I don't think anybody becomes a martyr simply because one expects a reward or fears punishment. I don't think anybody behaves heroically for such a reason.

All of the Church's martyrs were impelled by feelings of loyalty, because they believed strongly in something. The idea of the hereafter, where their actions would merit a reward, might have been of some help, but I don't think it was the main reason. People who do something out of fear generally fear the fire, the martyrdom and the torture even more. They don't dare to defy them. I think that throughout the Church's history, its martyrs must have been motivated by something more inspiring than fear or punishment. It's much easier for me to understand that.

We called for self-sacrifice and, at times, for martyrdom, heroism and death. I think it's a great merit for a person to give their life for a revolutionary idea and to fight, knowing they may die. Even though one knows there's nothing after death, one upholds the idea, the moral value, so firmly that one defends it with everything one has — without expecting a reward or punishment.

Basically, I would say that those were the weakest points in the religious teaching we were given. I don't think they produced many saints from among us. There weren't many boarding students in that school — only about 30 — and there were around 200 students in all. When I went on to the main Jesuit school, there were 1,000 students, 200 of whom were boarders. Not many priests must have come out of there. It would surprise me to know if even 10 priests came out of 1,000.

Awareness of social distinctions

Betto: Was there any social and racial discrimination?

Castro: Unquestionably. In the first place the institution itself was private. The Jesuits weren't motivated by profit, however. The Christian Brothers were not motivated by profit very much either, but they did attach some importance to the social prestige of money. Tuition wasn't expensive. Board at the Jesuit school in Santiago de Cuba cost 30 pesos a month. A peso was equal to a dollar at the time. I'm speaking of 1937, when I was 10 and a half or 11 years old.

That fee included room and board — the meals weren't bad — and outings. Some health care was also provided, and the students paid to join a cooperative medical society, a mutual benefit society. For anything more serious, we were sent to the hospital. We had water. Of course, if we wanted our clothes washed, we paid separately; textbooks were extra, too. But for classes, food, sports and everything else 30 pesos was not expensive, when you think of the personnel needed to cook, provide transportation and do the maintenance work for the school.

That was possible because those priests were not paid a salary. They were just fed; they lived very austerely. There were some lay teachers — who, naturally, received a small salary — and a rigorous administration. Austere, strict, self-sacrificing and hard-working, the Jesuits contributed human effort, thereby cutting costs. If they had been men who earned salaries and all that, the tuition would not have been just 30 pesos. It would have been double or triple that, even though the purchasing power of money was much greater then.

But even so, 30 pesos was within the reach of only a few families in that society. Day students paid eight or 10 pesos, more or less. This means that for 20 pesos more I got everything else.

Betto: Were any of your schoolmates blacks?

Castro: Let me explain. To begin with, the school itself was very exclusive, confined to the few families from the countryside, where I was from, or from small towns in the province's interior who could pay for it. As I've said, there were around 200 day students from Santiago de Cuba and 30 boarders. Not many families could afford to send their children to school, because they also had to pay their travel and clothing expenses. It cost a family at least 40 pesos a month. If the child got some money for buying ice cream, candy or something like that, it could cost as much as $50.

Therefore, the institution, as a private school, was the privilege of a small minority, and the students boarding there were the sons of businessmen and landowners — moneyed people. A worker's son or even the son of a professional — could not have gone there as a boarder, though he could have gone as a day student if he lived in Santiago de Cuba. But a teacher could not afford to send a child to one of those schools, because a teacher earned around $75. Many doctors and lawyers could not send their children. They would have had to have been eminent — very eminent — lawyers or doctors to have been able to send a child to those schools. Usually, only a family that had an estate, a factory, a coffee processing plant, a shoe factory, a distillery, or some other important business could send a child there.

I can remember the social origins of almost all my schoolmates there, both day students and boarders. Of course, if a family lived in Santiago de Cuba, there was no need for the child to board. A bus picked him up every morning and took him home in the evening. A family with a more modest income could pay the fees charged for a day student: $8-$10.

Those schools were very exclusive; they were upper-class schools, but even then there were two categories: the children of businessmen, manufacturers and professionals who lived in Santiago de Cuba proper, and those who lived in the rich Vista Alegre section — the middle bourgeoisie and the very rich bourgeoisie. The very rich bourgeoisie had an aristocratic spirit. They considered themselves different from the rest of us — superior. So in that exclusive school the division was not entirely based on money, though money lay at the root of it; rather it was based on social status, the houses where they lived and tradition.

My family may have had as many resources as some of those in that social group, but fortunately I wasn't in that category. Why not? Because my family lived in the countryside. There we lived among the people, the workers, all of whom were very poor. As I told you, we even had animals under the house — the cows, pigs, chickens and all that.

I was not the grandson or great-grandson of a landowner. Sometimes an old land-holding family did not have money any more, but kept the aristocratic or rich oligarchic class culture. Since my mother and father had been very poor farmers who managed to acquire some money and accumulate some wealth, my family did not have this culture as yet. They were people who worked every day in harsh conditions. They had no social life and hardly any relations with people like themselves. I think that if I had been the grandson or great-grandson of a landowner I might possibly have had the misfortune of acquiring that class culture, mentality and consciousness. I might not have had the privilege of escaping bourgeois ideology.

There was a whole group of students at that school who had that bourgeois, aristocratic mentality. They looked down on the other rich children who were less ostentatious about it. I did not attach much importance to this, but I noticed it. And I noticed that those in the second group competed with the very rich ones and held themselves apart. Even among the rich students, there were divisions that led to rivalry. I was perfectly well aware of that.

You had to be relatively rich to be at that school at all, and you breathed in an awareness of class distinction, the bourgeois institution and privilege. It wasn't a school for workers, proletarians or poor farmers — not even for professionals, except for the very exclusive ones.

There were, however, some black students at the La Salle School. In that regard it was more democratic. There were no black students at the Dolores College; all were supposedly white. This often puzzled me, both there and at the Havana school that I attended later on. I wondered why there were no black students. I remember that the only answer I was given was, "Well, it's really because there are very few of them, and a black child here among so many white ones would feel bad." So, in order to keep them from feeling bad, it wasn't a good idea to have one or two black children together with 20, 30 or 100 white ones. That was the argument I was given. I asked several times and always got the same answer. I did not know that racial discrimination existed. How could anybody who was still in the sixth grade — especially if he wasn't from a worker's family or a family that could explain the problem to him — have known about it? I asked why there weren't any black children out of sheer curiosity. I was given an explanation and I accepted it more or less.

I don't remember seeing even one black student while I was there. They might not even have accepted a mulatto. Of course, they did not do a blood test on everybody who entered the school, as Adolf Hitler's SS would have demanded; but, if you did not look white, you did not get in. I don't know how many cases there were or if any families challenged this. I had no way of knowing how many students were rejected because they weren't pure white.

But that's another matter; that enters the sociopolitical realm. In short, the schools were exclusive. I can talk about their good and bad aspects without bitterness. I feel grateful to those teachers and institutions, because they did not frustrate some positive things I had in me but, on the contrary, developed them. Personal factors, personal circumstances also influenced me a lot. I think that humans are the product of struggle and difficulties, that problems gradually mold a person in the same way that a lathe shapes a piece of material — in this case, the matter and spirit of a human being.

At that school, on my own, I decided to go on to the Jesuits' school in Havana. I had had no conflicts at Dolores College; I was successful academically and in sports. I had no problems in the sixth or seventh grades or in the first and second year of high school, as I was there until the end of the year; but I consciously decided to seek new horizons. I may have been influenced by the prestige of the other school in Havana, by its brochures and buildings, and the books written about it. I felt motivated to leave the school I was in and go to the other one. I made the decision and suggested it at home, and I was allowed to transfer to the other school, Belén College. It belonged to the Havana Jesuits and was the best Jesuit school in the country — perhaps the best school in Cuba in general, because of its material base and facilities. It was a huge place, a center with great prestige, attended by the cream of the aristocracy and the Cuban bourgeoisie.

After the triumph of the revolution, the school became a technological institute, and now it's a college of military technology, at the university level. It's a huge center and has been enlarged. For a while, it was a technological institute, but because of the need to develop the armed forces, we decided to locate there the Military Technological Institute, known as the ITM.

Belén College

When I was a student, there were around 200 boarders, a total of 1,000 students, including boarders and day students. It was a little more expensive, around $50 a month. It had more lay people, much more space, and higher expenses. The food may even have been better, and there were excellent sports fields. I think that $50 was cheap for that institution. I say "dollars" because with the current inflation in Latin America, nobody knows what a peso means. Once again the spirit of self-sacrifice and Jesuit austerity made relatively low fees possible.

The Jesuits' spirit of self-sacrifice and austerity, the kind of life they led, their work and their efforts made a school of that caliber possible at that price. A school like that in the United States today could cost $500 a month. There were several basketball courts, baseball fields, track and field facilities, volleyball courts, and even a swimming pool. It was a wonderful school.

I was a little older then, a junior in high school. I had never been to the capital of the republic. I went to Birán for my summer vacation and was given some money for buying clothes and other things. I also had to buy textbooks, pay my tuition and other expenses. I packed my suitcase and went off to Havana for the first time.

Betto: How old were you?

Castro: I had just turned 16. I joined the basketball team and some other teams in the 16-year-old age group. I began to take an active part in sports and became quite good in basketball, soccer, baseball and track and field — nearly everything — right from the start. When I arrived, I found a wide range of activities available. My favorites were sports and the Explorers. I maintained my old love of the mountains, camping and things like that, which I continued to do on my own. There was an Explorers' group there. It seems that during our first excursions, the teachers decided I was good, and they promoted me; then, one day they made me the head of the school's Explorers — the Explorers' general, as it was called.

The Explorers was a group not exactly like, but similar to, the Boy Scouts. We had our own uniforms and went camping in the wilderness, using tents. We used to go for one or two days. We had to do guard duty and things like that, and I added some other activities, such as mountain climbing.

While at this school, I climbed the highest mountain in the west. We had a three-day holiday, and I organized a trip to Pinar del Río Province with three of my friends. The expedition lasted five days instead of three, because the mountain was in the north and I did not know where it was exactly. We went out to look for it and to explore it. We took a train that went south, but the mountain was in the north. We began the trip at night and hiked for three days before reaching the mountain — Pan de Guajaibón, which was quite a difficult one to climb. We reached the top but got back to school two days after classes had started. Everyone was worried, because they did not know if we were lost or if something had happened to us.

During that period I was very active, mainly in sports, the Explorers and mountain climbing. I did not know — nor could I have imagined then — that I was preparing myself for the revolutionary struggle. And I studied. That was always a question of honor. It was not that I was a model student. I wasn't, because my interest in sport and activities of that kind meant that I spent a lot of time either taking part in sport or thinking about it. But I attended classes punctually and was disciplined. I paid attention — sometimes more, sometimes less. I always had a lot of imagination, and sometimes I managed to escape mentally from class and go around the world, being completely unaware of what the teacher was saying for the next 45 minutes. I now think the teachers were partly responsible.

Since I was an athlete, and a somewhat outstanding one, they were not as strict with me during the competition times as they were at other times. When the glories of the championships, medals and contests had faded away — competitions and rivalry were part of the history, prestige and name of schools of that kind — then they became demanding. Of course, I'm referring to the academic side, because they were generally very strict with regard to the students' behavior.

Several priests were very highly trained scientists, people who were very knowledgeable in physics, chemistry, mathematics and literature, though they were still very backward politically. I'm referring to a period from 1942 to 1945. I graduated from high school in 1945, when World War II ended. A few years earlier, the Spanish Civil War had ended, and all those priests (and the ones who hadn't yet been ordained but who were already teaching) were Nationalists — or, more frankly, pro-Franco — politically speaking. Except for a very few Cubans, they were all Spaniards. Just after the Spanish Civil War, there was a lot of talk about the horrors of the war, about Nationalists — even priests — who had been shot by firing squads. Very little was said about the communists and other Republicans who had been shot. It seems that the Spanish Civil War was very bloody, and there were excesses on both sides.

Betto: Was that the first time you heard about communism?

Castro: Well, I had been hearing for some time that communism was a terrible thing. Communism was always described in those terms.

All those Jesuits were rightists. Some were obviously kind people who expressed solidarity with others; they were exemplary in many ways. But, ideologically, they were right-wing, pro-Franco reactionaries. There was not even one left-wing Jesuit in Cuba at that time. I know that there are many left-wing Jesuits now, and I think you could point to some examples in the past. But at the school where I studied, just after the Spanish Civil War, there wasn't a single left-wing Jesuit. It was the worst period of all in that regard.

I took note of this, but did not question it very much. As I said, I was involved in sports. I was also trying to do well in my studies. Even though I wasn't a model student I felt morally obligated to pass all my exams. For me it was a question of honor. In general, I got good grades, even though my attention wandered in class and I had the bad habit of depending on last-minute cramming. We criticize this now and rightly so.

I had some duties at school, because students used to be assigned specific tasks. If you were in charge of a classroom or study hall, you had to turn out the lights and close the doors and windows. I was in charge of the main study hall where we stayed for a while after dinner before going to bed. During exam time, I had to be the last to leave. I used to stay there for two, three or four hours, going over my notes.

Even though it wasn't exactly right, it was allowed — perhaps because it did not hurt anybody. During exam time I studied all the time — before and after lunch and during recess. I studied the textbooks to learn everything I needed to know but didn't about mathematics, physics, chemistry and biology. I'm self-taught in all those subjects; somehow I managed to understand them. I developed a capacity to unravel the mysteries of physics, geometry, mathematics, botany and chemistry with textbooks alone. I usually got excellent grades, which were often higher than those obtained by the best students. Teachers from state institutes came to give us the examinations, and the school was very interested in the results.

Betto: What were those institutes?

Castro: The state high schools. Don't forget that this was during World War II when People's Fronts had been created, and some countries enacted laws to regulate their educational systems. Our 1940 constitution included some advances regarding education and lay schools, and according to Cuban law, the private schools which clearly served the more privileged sectors of the population had to comply with the law and follow the state high schools' program. There was only one program, and when the teachers in the state high schools — who had their pride, self-esteem and prestige as educators to maintain — came to test those privileged students in the Jesuit and other private schools, they gave hard exams, some more so than others. Perhaps some of them were more understanding than others. That was the time, I repeat, of the People's Fronts and the antifascist alliance. The Communist Party, which had already participated in drawing up the 1940 constitution, exerted some influence on the government later on and contributed to the ratification of some laws.

So the teachers came to give their exams, which were usually tough. It seems that my speciality was those exams given by the state teachers. Often when the best students became confused and did not answer correctly, I managed to get the highest grades in subjects that were considered difficult. I remember when I got the only high grade on a Cuban geography exam; it was 90. Our school complained to the state high school teachers, pointing to the low marks and they replied, "The textbook the students used isn't very good." Then our teachers said, "Well, there's one student who used that same textbook and got a 90." The thing is, I used a little imagination and made an effort to explain the answer. For me, the exams were a question of honor.

In short, I was very involved in sports, the Explorers and all kinds of outdoor activities; by cramming for exams during that period, I got good grades.

I also made a lot of friends among my fellow students. Without trying — and without even realizing it — I became popular as a sports enthusiast, an athlete, an Explorer, a mountain climber and also as an individual who, in the end, got good grades. Some political virtues may also have been apparent without my being aware of them.

Religious training

I went on religious retreats during that period. It goes without saying that the religious training remained the same as what I've already described about Dolores College. The same system prevailed, even though we were studying logic and philosophy.

We went on religious retreats for three days every year. Sometimes they were held at school, but sometimes we went somewhere else. All the students in the same grade were isolated for three days for religious lectures, meditation, spiritual communion and silence. Silence was the cruelest part. All of a sudden you had to become a mute and not say a word. Even so, that stillness had some pleasant aspects. I remember that so much philosophizing gave me a tremendous appetite. As a result, lunch and dinner were two wonderful hours; that gave me a lot of pleasure and satisfaction. The spiritual exercises began early.

Naturally, I had to go to mass every day in those schools. This was another policy that I think was negative: forcing students to go to mass every day.

Betto: At Dolores as well as Belén?

Castro: Yes. I don't remember what it was like at La Salle but I remember clearly that we had to go to mass every day at Dolores and Belén.

Betto: In the morning?

Castro: Yes, before breakfast. Every day we had the same ritual; I think it was quite mechanical. Having to go to mass every day was overdoing it, and I don't think it helps a child.

Along with mass there were prayers. As I see it now, repeating the same prayers over and over, saying the Hail Mary and the Our Father mechanically, had no positive effect; that's the best I can say. How many times I must have said them in the course of all those years! Did I ever stop to think what the prayer meant? Later on I noticed a form of praying in other religions in which the person seemed to be talking spontaneously with somebody; you use your own words and ideas to make a plea or a request, to express your will or feelings. They never taught us that; rather, they just told us to repeat the written words, to repeat them absolutely mechanically — 1, 10, 50 or 100 times. To me, that's not really praying. It may be good exercise for the vocal cords, the voice or whatever, of patience, if you will — but it's not praying.

Often I had to recite the litany in Latin and Greek, and I did not know what the words meant: "Kyrie eleison, Christe eleison." One person would say the litany and another would respond: "Ora pro nobis," etc. I almost remember the litany. We did not know what it meant or what we were saying; we just kept on repeating it mechanically. Over the years we grew accustomed to it. I tell you quite frankly that that was a great defect in the religious training I received.

When we were 16, 17 or 18, our spiritual exercises included meditation. During those three days of the religious retreat we meditated on philosophical and theological topics, but usually the theme was punishment — which, in the circumstances, was more far more likely — and reward. The reward did not inspire our imagination, but the punishment was described in such a way as to do just that.

I remember long sermons for meditation on hell — the heat and suffering, anguish and desperation it caused. I don't know how such a cruel hell as the one that was described to us could have been invented, because such severity is inconceivable, no matter how great a person's sins may have been. Moreover, the punishment for venial sins was way out of proportion. Even to doubt some dogma that you didn't understand was a sin. You had to believe it, because if you didn't, and had a fatal accident or died while in that state of sin, you could be condemned to hell. There was really no proportionality between the individual's sins and eternal punishment.

The idea was to arouse the imagination. I still remember an example that was often given in those spiritual exercises. There was always some written material, some theses or commentaries. We were told, "So you may have an idea of eternity, my children, imagine a steel ball the size of the world" — and I tried to imagine a steel ball the size of the world, with a circumference of 40,000 kilometers — "whose surface is grazed by the proboscis of a fly once every 1,000 years. Well, the fly will wear away the steel ball — that is, that steel ball the size of the world will disappear as a result of the fly's slight touch once every 1,000 years — before hell ends, and even after that, it will go on forever." That was the nature of our meditation, which I would describe as a form of mental terrorism; sometimes those explanations turned into mental terrorism.

It's near the end of the 20th century, and not so long ago, only 40 years — I'm amazed at what a relatively short time it is — one of the best schools in our country provided this kind of education. I don't think it was a good way to foster religious feeling.

Betto: Was the Bible mentioned a lot?

Castro: It was mentioned, but not very much. The meaning of a parable or a passage from the Gospels might be explained. We just kept on studying biblical history throughout that period. The editions of the book were larger every year. That is, we started with a slender volume and each year more subject matter was added. Biblical history was always in the curriculum and was very interesting. I always liked biblical history because its content was fascinating; it was wonderful for children and adolescents to know everything that had happened from the creation of the world to the Flood.

There's something I've never forgotten about biblical history. I'm not sure if it's actually mentioned in the Bible or not, but if it is, I think it will require some analysis. It's this: after the Flood one of Noah's sons — was it one of Noah's sons? — mocked his father. Noah made wine from grapes and drank so much that he became drunk. One of his sons made fun of him, and as a result his descendants were condemned to be black. I can't recall if the son mentioned in biblical history was Canaan. Who were Noah's sons?

Betto: Shem, Ham and Japheth. In the Bible, in Genesis, Canaan appears as the son of Ham — and therefore as one of Noah's offspring. Noah cursed Canaan and condemned him to be the last of the slaves. Since the slaves in Latin America were blacks, some old translations use the term *black* as a synonym for *slave*. Moreover, Canaan's descendants became the peoples of Egypt, Ethiopia and

Arabia, who are dark-skinned. But in the Bible his descendants weren't included in the curse, unless you make a slanted interpretation in order to seek religious justification for apartheid.

Castro: Well, I was taught that one of Noah's sons was punished by having black descendants. Somebody should check to see if this is being taught today and if it's really proper for a religion to teach that being black is a punishment of God. I remember that problem in biblical history.

All those stories fascinated me: the building of the ark, the Flood, all the animals, the landing of the ark, what life was like, Moses's travails, the crossing of the Red Sea, the promised land and all the wars and battles described in the Bible. I think I first learned about war in biblical history. That is, I became interested in the art of warfare. I was fascinated by it from Joshua's destroying the walls of Jericho to the sound of trumpets, to Samson's Herculean strength, which allowed him to tear a temple down with his bare hands. Those deeds were really fascinating. The entire period covered by the Old Testament was marvelous: Jonah and the whale that swallowed him, the punishment dealt to Babylon and the prophet Daniel. Of course, we could have studied other stories, those of other peoples and their interpretations, but I believe that few are as fascinating as the ones in the Old Testament and biblical history.

After biblical history came the New Testament with its many parables. These were repeated and generally explained to us with the terms used in the Bible, which were interesting. The crucifixion and death of Christ with all the explanations that were given always had an impact on children and young people.

Sympathy for the poor

Betto: When did you begin to feel sympathy with the cause of the poor?

Castro: I'll have to go into my childhood experiences. First of all, where I was born and raised, we lived among poor people; all of the children went barefoot. I realize now they must have had a lot of hardships. I now think of the diseases that struck them and their suffering. I was not aware of all this then, but we had a very close relationship. They were my friends and comrades in everything. We went to the river, the woods and the fields together to hunt and to play. During my vacations, they were my friends and buddies. I did not belong to another social class. We were always together. I had a very free life there.

There was no bourgeois or feudal society in Birán. There were not even 20 or 30 landowners whose families would get together, always forming the same group. My father was an isolated landowner. Sometimes a friend would visit him, but we hardly ever visited anybody. My parents usually stayed home; they did not go to visit other families. They worked all the time. So, the only people we saw were the ones who lived there. I used to go to the Haitians' quarters, to their huts; sometimes I was scolded for this, but only because I ate the dry corn they cooked. I got into trouble for health, not social reasons, because I ate with them. Nobody at home ever said, "Don't go near so-and-so." Never. They weren't class conscious; they did not have rich people's or landowners' mentality.

I was not aware of the privilege of having many things. My family had everything and was always treated with respect, but I was raised with these people without any prejudices or bourgeois culture or ideology. This must have had an influence.

Ethical values came from my education, that is, from school, from the teachers and, I would say, from my family, from home. I was told very early in life that I should never lie. There were clear ethical values. They weren't Marxist and they did not stem from an ethical philosophy. They were based on a religious ethic. I was taught what was right and wrong, things that should and should not be done. In our society, the first notion children got of ethical principles may have been based on religion. In the prevailing religious environment, people absorbed a number of ethical values as a matter of tradition, including some irrational beliefs, such as believing that the flight and screeching of an owl or the crowing of a rooster could foretell disaster.

Later on, my experiences in life began to create a feeling of what was wrong, the violation of an ethical standard, a sense of injustice, abuse or fraud. So, I received not only a set of ethical values, but also some experience of the violation of ethical standards and what unethical people were like. I began to have an idea of what was fair and unfair. I also began to develop a concept of personal dignity. It would be very difficult to give a complete explanation of what a sense of personal dignity is based on. There may be people who are more sensitive than others to this. A person's character also has an influence. Why is one person more rebellious than another? I think that the conditions in which someone is educated can make them more rebellious or less rebellious. Character and temperament also play a role. Some people are more docile, more receptive to discipline and more obedient than others. But the fact remains that you gradually develop a sense of justice, of what is fair and what is unfair.

In this regard, from very early on I think I've had a sense of justice, because of what I saw and experienced. I also feel that physical exercise and participation in sports can teach us a lot: rigor, endurance, determination and self-discipline.

Undoubtedly, my teachers, my Jesuit teachers, especially the Spanish Jesuits, who inculcated a strong sense of personal dignity — regardless of their political ideas — influenced me. Most Spaniards are endowed with a sense of personal honor, and it's very strong in the Jesuits. They valued character, rectitude, honesty, courage and the ability to make sacrifices. Teachers definitely have an influence. The Jesuits clearly influenced me with their strict organization, their discipline and their values. They contributed to my development and influenced my sense of justice — which may have been quite rudimentary but was at least a starting point.

Following this path I came to view abuse, injustice and the humiliation of a fellow human as unthinkable. These values were developed gradually in my conscience and stayed with me. Several things contributed to my developing a certain set of ethical values, and life itself kept me from acquiring a class culture, a sense of belonging to a different, superior class. I think this was the basis from which I later developed political consciousness.

If you mix ethical values with a spirit of rebellion and rejection of injustice, you begin to appreciate and place a high value on a number of things that other people don't value at all. A sense of personal dignity, honor and duty form the main foundation that enables people to acquire political consciousness. This was especially so in my case, since I did not acquire it by having poor, proletarian, or farm origins — that is, through social circumstance. I gained my political consciousness through reasoning, thinking, by developing feelings and deep conviction.

I think that what I was telling you about faith — the ability to reason, think, analyze, meditate and develop feelings — is what makes it possible to acquire revolutionary ideas. In my case, there was a special circumstance: nobody taught me political ideas. I did not have the privilege of having a mentor. Most of the people who have played a role in our history had mentors, outstanding teachers or professors. Unfortunately, I've had to be my own mentor all my life. How grateful I would have been if somebody had taught me about politics, if somebody had taught me revolutionary ideas!

Nobody could instill religious faith in me through the mechanical, dogmatic and irrational methods that were employed. If somebody asked me if I had ever held religious beliefs, I would have to say: never, really. I never really held a religious belief or had religious faith. At school, nobody ever managed to instill those values in me. Later on, I had other values: a political belief, a political faith, which I forged on my own, as a result of my experience, analysis and sentiments.

Political ideas are worthless if they aren't inspired by noble, selfless sentiments. Likewise, noble sentiments are worthless if they aren't based on correct, fair ideas. I'm sure that the same pillars that sustain the sacrifices a revolutionary makes today sustained the sacrifices made in the past by a martyr who died for their religious faith. I think that religious martyrs were generous, selfless people; they were made of the same stuff of which revolutionary heroes are made. Without those qualities, there can be no religious or political heroes.

I've had to continue on my way — a long way — to develop my revolutionary ideas, and they have the immense value of being conclusions reached on my own.

2

University Days

Without a doubt, it was a privilege to enter this university, because I learned a lot here; it was here that I learned what may have been some of the most important things in my life. Here I discovered the greatest ideas of our epoch and of our times. Here I became a revolutionary and a devotee of [José] Martí. Here I became a socialist — initially a utopian socialist — thanks to the lectures of Professor Delio, who gave classes in political economy (and it was capitalist political economy, so difficult to understand and yet so easy to expose in its irrationality and its absurd aspects). That's why I was initially a utopian socialist, although thanks also to my contacts with political literature, here in the university and at law school, I subsequently became a Marxist-Leninist.

I lived through difficult moments in this university, very difficult, so much so that it is purely by chance that I survived those university years. I engaged in very hard struggles, with all the necessary persistence and determination, until other years and other epochs arrived.

First political experience

I have to say that when I entered the university, I knew very little about politics. What did I know about politics at that time? What I most remember is that I had a brother, or a half-brother, running as a

---

Fifty years after he entered the University of Havana in 1945 to study law, Fidel Castro gave this speech to a meeting in the Aula Magna (Great Hall) of the University of Havana on September 4, 1995.

candidate with the Authentic Party,[1] there in Oriente Province. I remember that at that time there were 42 representatives for Oriente Province and each party fielded its candidates. I would probably have been about 14 years old and I went around the huts and houses in Birán teaching people how to vote. I taught them how to vote for Pedro Emilio Castro. I don't remember his exact number on the voting slip, but I had to explain to those people, almost all of whom were illiterate, where to go, about the party and everything, and where they had to put their *X*.

I was not a revolutionary at the age of 14, nor was I political or made a particular political choice; the candidate was my brother and he had promised me a horse if he won in the elections. In reality, I had very little interest in that campaign back in 1939. But he used to talk to me, and he was kind enough to discuss things with me. Young people always like to be in touch with things, to be taken seriously, and he gave me that task which I kept at until election day. But all my efforts came to nothing as the Rural Guards arrived and prevented everyone from voting.

Maybe I need to make some historical rectification as to the exact year of that election — maybe it was earlier. I may not even have been 14 years old when I did that political campaigning for Pedro Emilio as the first alternate candidate among the representatives for that party. However, it would have been a matter of luck if one of the representatives had happened to die and Pedro Emilio entered the House of Representatives and kept his promise to buy me a horse. You have to understand the significance of his promise to me: I believe it was an Arabian horse. This was my first political experience.

Those elections were decided by force, because in real terms the Authentic Party had an overwhelming majority. The soldiers arrived, set up two lines, those voting in favor of the government on one side and those against the government on the other; the former voted and the latter did not. That happened in all the polling places, especially in the rural areas. That was how they held the elections and that was my first experience with elections.

I remember a great bitterness when I saw how they attacked the people there, mistreated them, assaulted them, and thus I witnessed

---

[1] The Cuban Revolutionary (Authentic) Party was founded in June 1934 by Ramón Grau San Martín and other opponents of ex-President Machado.

my first great political farce, the first fraudulent elections I saw.

Later, the same thing happened in the presidential elections, and in this way [Fulgencio] Batista gained the presidency of the republic in 1940.[2] Batista really was a strongman, an abuser of authority. The military ruled; everything was at the service of the big companies, of the big estates, of the major interests. They received all the privileges and all kinds of sinecures.

There was tremendous abuse in the rural areas. It is incredible that a situation like that could have been maintained for such a long period, with a few Rural Guards from the army created after the dissolution of the Liberation Army, with its U.S. uniforms, its U.S. machetes, its U.S. rifles and Texas horses. That army created terror in all the rural areas of our country, which explains the fatal situation of our peasants and our agricultural workers, who went hungry and were unemployed most of the time.

Reflections on childhood
In my childhood, I had the opportunity of living among very poor families. We went around with and played with their children. I thought a lot about that much later. Throughout my life I have remembered what I saw as a child. Perhaps those images, those memories and impressions awoke in me a certain sympathy and solidarity toward those people.

Throughout my life, the special circumstances of the place where I was born and my parents' occupation forced decisions on me. You wouldn't believe me if I told you that I took my first decision when I was in first grade, when I had to persuade the family that was looking after me in Santiago de Cuba to allow me to be a first grade boarder in the La Salle School, which I had been attending as a day pupil. This is how I came to be a first grade boarder at the school.

In the fifth grade I had to make another decision, to leave that school, principally over issues of abuse by teachers, especially physical violence against my person, which also obliged me to use violence against a certain inspector. I don't want to mention names,

---

[2] Batista had led the "Sergeants' revolt" in September 1933. In elections widely viewed as rigged, he became president from 1940 to 1944. He then left Cuba to live in the United States, returning in 1948. On March 10, 1952, General Batista led a military coup, which overthrew the Authentic Party's government of President Carlos Prío. Batista finally fled Cuba in January 1959 following the victory of the revolutionary forces led by Fidel Castro.

1928. Fidel Castro, aged 20 months at his home in Birán.

1929. Fidel Castro at 3 years.

1936. La Salle College in Santiago de Cuba. Fidel is in the second row, third from the right, standing behind his brother Raúl.

1940. Santiago de Cuba, in the house of his sister Lidia.

Dolores College, 1940. Fidel Castro is standing (front row, second from left).

Top: Vacation in Pinares de Mayarí, 1937, on a tractor.
Below: Fidel Castro, 13, (right) at Dolores College, 1940.

1941. Dolores College, Santiago de Cuba.

1941. Fidel (left), Raúl (center) and Ramón Castro (right) at Dolores College, Santiago de Cuba.

Hunting while on vacation in Birán, December 1943.

Graduation photo, 1945,
Belén College, Havana.
© Ocean Press/Cuban Council of State

Fidel Castro giving a speech at Belén College.
© Ocean Press/Cuban Council of State

Member of Belén College's basketball team, 1943.

Fidel Castro (left) in Bogotá, Colombia, 1948.

1947. Fidel Castro (right) at the office of the Federation of University Students (FEU).

Speaking as an organizer of the Orthodox Party Youth.

Fidel Castro, 1951. Photo used as Orthodox Party candidate.

Fidel Castro campaigning as Orthodox Party candidate, 1951.

because those things belong to the past. I had to rebel and physically fight when I was in fifth grade, in the early part of that year.

From there, I went to Dolores College. There things were a bit hard for me, though there is no need to go into the history of all that. In spite of having reached a better school, I could more or less respond to the demands of that institution. Once again I had been sent as a day student rather than a boarder so that, a little later, I had to engage in a third battle to become a boarding student.

I went there in fifth grade, and I was there until the second year of high school — they had already increased the program from four years to five. Then I decided to leave there for Belén College, which was the best Jesuit school in this country. The idea of this school attracted me. I felt more suited to the Jesuit discipline and their behavior in general.

At that time I did a lot of sports. From a young age I liked scaling mountains. On every outing to El Cobre or similar places, I used to get lost trying to climb some of the mountains that I saw on the horizon; or if there were torrential downpours, to cross swollen rivers. I enjoyed all those kinds of adventures. The teachers were tolerant. Sometimes I came back late, kept the bus waiting for two hours, and they did not create a big fuss.

So later, when I moved on to another academy, I was in the best physical shape to practice a lot of sports, especially mountain climbing. All that came from Belén College.

Was I a good student? No, I was not a good student. I have to start by telling you that I can't present myself to this generation as a good student. I attended my classes, that's certainly true, as Professor Delio has said — not without some displeasure on his part, because he would have liked me to have been a model student in everything. The teacher was in my classroom over here, and I would have my mind elsewhere. The teacher would be explaining a subject, and I would be thinking about who knows what — about mountains, or sports, or whatever else boys and girls think about.

Subsequently, I became a last-minute crammer, which is the worst recommendation you could give to anyone. Well, I was a good finalist. In that, I think I could perhaps compete with Ana Fidelia in that recent race when she won the world championship.[3] At the last

---

[3] Ana Fidelia Quirot is an outstanding Cuban track and field athlete.

minute I devoted all my time to studying: during recreation, lunch, dinner, as a self-taught student.

I studied mathematics, physics and science by myself as the end of the course approached; and in the end, I obtained good grades, way above the top students of the year, due to my last-minute effort. The Jesuit teachers really praised my efforts in this championship period; they forgave me for everything and judged me at the end of the course, after they had written to my folks saying that I would surely fail.)

I will never forget one teacher with a very strong character. He was an inspector who called me up one time, having contacted the man who was my guardian and having told him that I was failing the course. I'm not sure if this was the second year out of the three years I spent there. I studied as I had always done — at the last minute — and I remember one day when I was leaving the dining room the same severe inspector said to me, with a Spaniard's accent: "Do you know what grade you achieved in physics?"

Even though I knew that I had done well on the test, I thought that there was something behind this question; so I acted the fool and replied: "No." He said, "One hundred!" The top pupil had achieved 90 — the school genius had achieved 90 — when he took the institute examinations.

In Cuban geography, of all the students, only one achieved 90, and I had that honor; everyone else got less. There was a great controversy between the school and the institute, about the books and the texts. What book had Castro studied from? In fact, I had studied from the same books as everyone else, but I also added things from my imagination. Not that I invented capes or bays or rivers, but I always added something of my own to the test, and for some reason he liked the test and gave me a grade of 90. But I would recommend against leaving all the studying to the end as I did.

No one ever managed to inculcate in me the habit of studying every day, and the fact is that they tolerated my behavior because of my sporting achievements. They treated me better than the Cuban national team. They did not criticize me until the end. They never really taught me how to study every day.

As mentioned, the school was run by Jesuits, Spaniards. The Spanish Republic had ended two or three years before and one of the teachers or aides, who was a good friend of mine, told me about the executions after the war. He had been a medic and told me long stories about the number of prisoners who were executed in Spain when the Civil War ended. It made me very indignant. He told me about it as if it were the most natural thing in the world. He made no criticisms of it, but the story he told was quite dramatic, considering everything that occurred. Logically, the teacher's political viewpoint was conservative, right-wing.

Technically the school was a good one in many things, but all the teaching was dogmatic. We mustn't forget that everyone had to go to mass and study religious history in the first and second year. The teaching was absolutely dogmatic. In general, there were some laboratories, some research, some other things; but the system of education needed to be revolutionized, because it did not really teach the students how to think. We had to believe things even if we did not really understand them. Not to believe was a sin worthy of hell.

I really don't have any desire to criticize that school, but I'm explaining the type of education we received, which was far from what is considered an ideal education for any young person today.

Otherwise, life was good for me at that school because of sports, explorations, excursions, all those things. I had good relations with all the boys, excellent relations. I know this because the day I finished school, they cheered when I was presented with my high school diploma.

I myself did not realize that I had so many friends at school. I think it was because of the kind of relationships I had with everyone, without politicking or anything like that. But when I got to the university, what did I know about politics?

What had I brought from that school, what had I brought from my home, what did I take to the university? A profound sense of justice, a certain ethic. That ethic had Christian precepts, which I learned fighting injustice from a very early age, with a sense of equality in my relationships from an early age, and undoubtedly because of a rebellious temperament, however you want to describe it. I reacted; I never resigned myself to abuse and the imposition of things by force.

Batista comes to power

When I enrolled in this university at the end of 1945, we were living through one of the worst epochs of the history of our country and also one of the most deceptive. I was actually living through the aftermath of a frustrated revolution, the revolution of 1933. The struggle against Machado[4] had turned into a real revolution.

September 4 is considered an ill-fated date, because that is when Batista[5] came to power. But September 4 was not an ill-fated but rather a revolutionary date. Today, we don't have to be ashamed to be starting the school year on this date because the sergeants simply rose up against all those compromised leaders. There were many revolutionaries in that movement; students even participated in that government, which removed all the old guard of the army from power. That is to say, Batista began his life with a revolutionary act.

The problems came later, when the United States started interfering. They intervened in the internal politics of Cuba and made Batista an instrument for their interests in this country. At first there was a government, which was later led by Grau San Martín,[6] a university physiology professor who got along very well with the students. Then they named a cabinet with Guiteras[7] in a very important position; a series of revolutionary measures were adopted by that government, which only lasted three months. The measures were worker-oriented, dealing with, for example, the electric company. I think this is when the electric company nationalization occurred, which was talked about for a long time after. A revolutionary government was formed which started to apply a series of laws until the United States toppled that government; that's when Batista's behind-the-throne role began. That is to say, he kept on

---

[4] General Gerardo Machado Morales was president of Cuba from May 1925 to August 1933.

[5] Batista first gained power as a result of leading the "Sergeants' Revolt" in September 1933 against the U.S.-mandated presidency of Carlos Manuel de Céspedes, which was opposed by the military, militant students and revolutionary groups.

[6] After the "Sergeants' Revolt," a junta, which included Ramón Grau San Martín, ran the country for five days, after which Grau was named president by the rebels. The United States, however, refused to recognize the government and pressured Batista to desert the rebels; supported by the U.S. Embassy, Batista overthrew Grau on January 15, 1934.

[7] Antonio Guiteras was one of the leaders of the 1933 revolution and a fervent anti-imperialist. As part of the provisional government, he issued many anti-imperialist decrees and nationalist and social reform measures, including the eight-hour day and minimum-wage laws. Following the January 1934 coup, Batista carried out fierce repression in which thousands of revolutionaries were murdered, including Guiteras.

removing and replacing different governments and maintained power for 11 years, until 1944. They committed all kinds of abuses, crimes and thefts. No one knows how much those people stole, how much they extract-ed from this country! He was the puppet of the United States.

Later that revolution was frustrated. Then came the big struggles. There was the strike of March 1935, an attempt to overthrow the government, which was repressed mercilessly by Batista's government. They sowed terror in the city and the countryside and frustrated the revolution. It's hard to determine the aftereffects of a frustrated revolution and the political process that followed.

Then came a complicated international situation: the rise of fascism, with Hitler acquiring tremendous power in Europe and arming himself to the hilt. At the same time, the Soviet Union was following a purge policy with all kinds of abuses and crimes. Of course, all this came out later, after Khrushchev's denunciations in the 1950s, after Stalin died. They practically decapitated the party and the armed forces. They decapitated everything and helped create the most adverse conditions when the war started, with the exception of the great industrialization effort.

Creation of the broad front

At that time the Communist International, the Comintern, was operating, outlining the policies for all the Communist parties in the world. They launched the slogan of a broad front in the face of the danger of fascism, a policy that all the Communist parties followed with great discipline — we could say with exemplary discipline — creating a new situation.

Batista also started to call himself antifascist and he agreed with the creation of this broad front. The Communist Party had a very disciplined participation in this broad front policy. I'm not making a historical judgment, far from it. Maybe it's up to the researchers and historians to consider whether under these circumstances, another alternative was possible. It was an unquestionably correct policy on the outside, because what allowed Hitler to come to power in Germany was the division among the German left, between the Social Democrats and the German Communist Party. In other words, perhaps an anti-Hitler policy should have begun to develop before, but in Cuba, a Marxist-Leninist party had to become allied with the bloody, repressive and corrupt government of Batista.

I say this because, in my judgment, it had political consequences in this country. While the army repressed the peasants, the workers and the students, the Communist Party, due to international commitments, still felt obliged to be allied to that government. Nevertheless, it must be said, that the party was tireless in its defense of the workers' interests. All of the strikes, all of the fundamental battles that took place in that period for better wages, to improve the living conditions of the population, were actually carried out by the Communist Party and the working-class Communist leaders with great loyalty and utter dedication. But many people were anti-Batista, many people repudiated the abuses, crimes and corruption. This contradiction logically led many young people, people with revolutionary tendencies and people on the left to stop looking favorably upon the Cuban Marxist-Leninist party. This is the objective historical reality.

After the war against fascism ended, the Cold War and the United States' fight against socialism began. The United States emerged from the world war with enormous power, much more wealth and with almost all of the world's gold hoarded away.

Around this time there was a change in the Cuban government: Batista lost the 1944 elections and Grau stepped into office. Many people were deluded into thinking that a government of the people, an honest — you could say almost revolutionary government — had finally arrived. But that administration had already been eroded by politicking and corruption.

One of the biggest frustrations of our country was what occurred a few months after the Grau administration came to power. Of course, in those days everyone called themselves revolutionaries, including those who had been against Machado, everyone who was around during the revolution of 1933, those who had been involved in the political strike and all the struggles over many years. Well, the politicians had the government, but there were many people who came from that group who called themselves revolutionaries.

University politics

One year after Grau's victory, I enrolled at the university, the protests about dirty business and misappropriations had already begun. Of course, the university was buzzing. Many of those who supported that government had been in the Revolutionary Directorate. They were ministers. There was a great deal of confusion.

When I got to the university I was really ignorant, and I must have seemed strange to the Communists. They would say: "Here's the son of a landowner and a graduate of Belén College — he should be a hard-core right-winger." I almost frightened the few Communists at the university. There were only a few good, very active, real fighters who were struggling under unfavorable conditions. The repression had already started to affect them due to the Cold War and the repression of Communists. They were becoming marginalized. There was a ferocious anticommunist campaign and propaganda in all the media, the radio and the newspapers, battering communism from every direction. Many of its most capable and self-sacrificing working-class leaders were later assassinated.

The anti-imperialist sentiment had grown much weaker, including in our university, which had been the bastion of anti-imperialism from the days of Mella,[8] to the epoch of Villena,[9] the times of the Directorate and the fight against Batista. I was a witness to all this. I talked with all kinds of people, law students, people in every faculty, and almost never heard anyone say anything anti-imperialist.

The university had become a bastion of Grau's young supporters. The authorities, all the national organizations of the police, the secret police, the bureau investigating enemy activities — whatever it was called — the national police, all these institutions were in Grau's hands. The army was used for the major repression of big strikes and such. But the police were in charge of most activities, including the university police force.

I practiced sports during my first few months at the university, because I wanted to continue with this. I also became interested in politics, not so much anything concerned with the world outside the university, just internal university politics.

I nominated myself as a candidate for anthropology delegate. This was a special subject because students could be helped in different ways, with information about the practicals, with advice about lab

---

[8] Julio Antonio Mella founded the Federation of University Students (FEU) in 1923 and the Communist Party in Cuba in 1925. Under General Machado's dictatorial presidency, Mella was imprisoned and led a hunger strike. Later freed, he went into exile in Mexico, where he was assassinated by an agent of the Batista dictatorship.

[9] Rubén Martínez Villena was a nationalist and anti-imperialist; together with Mella, Guiteras and Chibás (leader of the Orthodox Party), he opposed both Machado and Batista and established the revolutionary government of 1933–34.

days and exams; there were many students who were registered but did not come to the university to attend classes. I also organized the first-year candidacy. Naturally, there were second- and third-year students already trying to win us over so they would have the majority, because the delegates from different subjects in the same year elected the delegate of that year, and those delegates elected the president of the law school. That's how it was.

I began these activities during my first year, when I was also playing sports. Before long, I could see that I wouldn't be able to do both. Naturally, I dedicated myself totally to the political activities, organizing the candidacy, seeking support from other students. We worked well. We had to deal with some real slick politicos, but our work produced results.

I remember that on election day around 200 students went to vote. I pulled in 181 votes and my opponent got 33, and our group won in every subject and all the delegates of the first year. How was it in the final election? It was a united vote; the majority won and they elected me the class delegate. Somewhere around that time they also elected me school treasurer. To tell you the truth, this was strange because the law school did not have a single cent, so it was an honorary position, the treasurer of nothing. That's how I began in my first year.

Relatively speaking, I had already started to stand out. At the time, the credibility of the government had begun to deteriorate quickly and we students were protesting against that government.

The Chibás-led split within the Orthodox Party occurred around this time, in response to the frustration with Grau's government, resulting in the new Party of the Cuban People. [10] We had already been protesting against that government. The university leaders at that time had high government positions, cushy jobs and everything; they had all the resources of the government at their disposal.

So my struggle got harder the second year when the law school became decisive in the Federation of University Students [FEU] election. I did the same work the second year — working on the second and the first years at the same time, with the same policies.

---

[10] The Party of the Cuban People, also called the Orthodox Party, was founded in 1947 by Eduardo Chibás, a progressive leader of the reformist movement. Also a leader of the revolutionary movement in 1933, Chibás was highly respected for his campaigns against theft and corruption in government.

Our opponents could not get a candidacy together in the second-year class. So with the support of the first-year students, we had another landslide victory. We now had two classes. The government supporters took it upon themselves to control the FEU in every way, first by trying to win us and later by threatening us.

In those law school elections, my opponents were strong, and not all of them were pro-government. Because of this there was a certain division in the ranks. The result could have been otherwise; one fourth year individual (there were five years with each one having one vote) became decisive. He was elected president of the school, even though he was weak, because of his commitment to vote against the government's candidate in the FEU. I think I acted a little precipitously, somewhat carried away with the school's internal struggle; with a little more experience I would have sought the election of a more capable and loyal, unaligned candidate who was not necessarily pro-government either. Our candidate did not fulfill his commitment to vote against the government in the FEU, so we took it upon ourselves to remove him from office. We simply got together a majority of four years and pulled him out.

That is how the law school politics became a bone of contention and the decisive issue in the university.

As a consequence of the frustrated revolution there were several factions in Cuba that called themselves revolutionary, to which the media gave major coverage. They were generally accepted by an important sector of public opinion, for their activity in some previous event. All of them, of course, were tied to the government, although not without rivalry among themselves.

So I was all alone at the university, absolutely alone, when suddenly, in that university electoral process, I was faced with the whole mafia gang that dominated the university, who were bent on maintaining control of the university at all costs. They ran the rector's office, the university police, the city police, everything. They decided that the removal of the law students' president from office was invalid. Their argument was that there was nothing about removal from office in the statutes, in spite of the fact that there were important precedents involving the removal of their adversaries that had been accepted by these same authorities. The rector's office invalidated the removal of the law school president. Therefore this vote decided if the university would continue being in the hands of pro- or anti-government forces. That is the story.

All of this translated into great danger for me, because of the environment at the university. It was an environment of force, fear and guns. The group that dominated the university was closely linked to the government and had all the support, resources and arms of the government.

In what sense do I think that I acted prematurely? Perhaps I should have prolonged that confrontation. Nevertheless, I could not resist the attempts at intimidation and threats, and I found myself alone, in open combat with those forces. I had no organization to take them on, no party to support me. It was a rebellion against their attempt to subjugate the university and forcefully impose their will.

Barred from the university

Articles have been written about my university years. People have looked for materials, dates, everything. I'm not really satisfied with the articles, but I respect their right to publish them, and they are good enough. They have a lot of information, but there is a lot omitted, in general, about the situation.

Without going into great detail, the physical pressures on me were very strong, as were the threats. The FEU elections were approaching and that mafia gang forbade me from attending the university. I believe that Luisito Báez Delgado wrote an article saying that I went off to a beach in order to decide whether or not to return, and how I finally did.

I've told this story to my friends several times. Not only did I go to the beach to think, but I also cried at the age of 20 — not because I had been forbidden to return to the university but because, in any case, I was going to return. There was a whole gang of them there — I don't know how many — with the authorities behind them. They had everything on their side. So I decided to return, and I returned armed. One could say that it was the beginning of my own personal armed struggle because at that time armed struggle was almost impossible. I asked an older friend with an anti-Machado and anti-Batista background to find me a pistol, and he got me a 15-shot Browning. I felt extremely well armed with that gun because I was generally a good shot. I had lived in the countryside and had gained a lot of experience with the rifles we had at home, without anyone's permission, and with the revolvers and all types of weapons. It just happened that I became a good shot.

So why did I cry? I cried because I felt that I would have to sacrifice myself in any case. After the fight at the university in which I had the support of the university students, with great support — I'm referring to all those students in my year and the younger class, and the students from other schools — I had to face the challenge of being banned from the university. I made the decision and got myself a weapon. It pained me a lot to think that perhaps no one would recognize the merit of such a death, that our very enemies would write the history of what had happened. Nevertheless, I made the decision to return to the university. Not only that, but also to put up a good fight. We did not know how many adversaries there were who would have to pay along with myself. I decided to return. I had no doubts about what I had to do.

What prevented me from dying that day? The truth was that one friend had other friends, and there were various people, various organizations and lots of people armed everywhere — some were young, highly esteemed, courageous young men. My friend took the initiative as he had very good relations with the students and said to me, "You cannot sacrifice yourself like this." He persuaded another seven or eight to come with me, people whom I did not know. They were excellent. I have known men, fighters, but these were sound, valiant young men. So I did not go alone.

We met up there beside what was the cafeteria. The bullies and the mafia had gathered there, near the law school. So I said to the others: "You three go in at the front. Three of us will go up the staircase over there. Another three will approach from here." So we arrived there suddenly and the people there, about 15 to 20 of them, began to tremble. It had never crossed our minds that we could put up such a powerful challenge. On that occasion nothing happened, they just trembled. I went to the university and continued going to the university, but after that day I came back alone.

Sometimes I was armed, but this created another problem. They had the university police, the street police and all the repressive organizations. They also had the courts and Urgency Court. There was a law stipulating that if you had a weapon, you went to prison. So I found myself facing another dilemma: having to confront the mafia gang without being able to use arms, because if I did so, they would seize me and put me into prison. Those courts were very harsh, and one could be locked up on the slightest exhortation from the government. So I had to continue my fight against that armed band, almost always unarmed, because it was only in exceptional cases that I took a gun.

This battle around the university and its control by the government had to be carried out, we could say, unarmed. That's why I say that it was an armed fight which took place in very peculiar circumstances, in which on many occasions all I had was myself. Eventually they got tired of all that planning; chance and luck were very much the order of the day. On one occasion the whole anthropology class went with me to the place where I lived, surrounding me because I was unarmed, while the adversaries were organized and armed.

Those were the ups and downs of those times. The whole battle for the FEU was so tense that it was finally more or less resolved at the end of a meeting containing a mix of friends and enemies, and a compromise candidate was found. Then there was a certain period of reconciliation and calm.

The battle against Trujillo

It was in the middle of all this that the Cayo Confites expedition arose.[11] This was the middle of 1947, the end of my second year. I had already become the president of the Dominican Pro-Democracy Committee as well as of the Committee for the Liberation of Puerto Rico. There was great opposition to Trujillo[12] at the university and for the liberation of Puerto Rico. Albizu Campos[13] was around at that time and led many of the uprisings, giving rise to many large solidarity demonstrations.

---

[11] Cayo Confites, a key in northern Cuba, was the site of a camp in Oriente Province from which an armed expedition against the Dominican dictator Trujillo was planned in 1947. After a few months, the attack was called off and the expeditionary force never left Cuba. Its 1,500 Dominican and Cuban participants, of whom Fidel Castro was one, were imprisoned in Havana. Fidel Castro was one of the few who eluded arrest. After a hunger strike, all the prisoners were released.

[12] Rafael Trujillo Molina (1891–1961), a Dominican soldier, ran unopposed for president of the Dominican Republic in 1930 and controlled that country as dictator until he was assassinated in 1961. In 1946 he issued an amnesty to exiled communists, but when they returned he had them executed, after which the Cayo Confites expedition was planned.

[13] Pedro Albizu Campos was a Puerto Rican nationalist. He was leader of the Nationalist Party and of the Puerto Rican Independence Movement.

At the time there was an endless number of demonstrations at the Presidential Palace against the government. I was photographed standing at the wall of the Palace, making a speech against Grau. He wanted to talk to the representatives, but we did not want to have any contact with him. We were protesting against the killing of a student. I do not remember the exact circumstances as there were many protests just like that one.

But while we were waging these hard battles, those people became increasingly powerful. It was the era of Alemán,[14] the infamous BAGA coalition and unbridled thievery. All those groups that dominated the university supported Alemán who had political ambitions. They used the banner of the noble Dominican cause.

It was around that time that the conditions were thought to be ready for the organization of the final onslaught against Trujillo; apart from the Dominicans themselves, many of these people [in Cuba] organized the Cayo Confites expedition. Alemán, the Education Minister, supplied most of the funds. It was one of the most badly organized things I have ever seen in my life. They rounded up people from the streets of Havana, paying no heed to their level of education, political awareness and knowledge in general. They simply wanted to organize an artificial army as quickly as possible. They got together about 1,200 men.

Naturally, seeing that the battle against Trujillo was about to begin and being the president of the Dominican Pro-Democracy Committee, I did not think twice. I packed my bags, and without saying anything to anyone, went to Cayo Confites to enlist in that expedition.

Perhaps the most important factor in all of this was that I signed up alongside the vast majority of my enemies. Curiously, they respected me. If there was one thing I learned throughout those years when I had to look death in the face, unarmed on many occasions, it is that the enemy respects those who do not fear him, those who challenge him. The action I took of doing my duty as a student won their respect. That's the way it was.

While I was there in Cayo Confites, at the final stage, everything

---

[14] Julián Alemán was Minister of Education in the government of Grau San Martín and engaged in flagrant corruption and graft, including misuse of education funds. He was a key target of the anti-Grau forces and was later murdered by the Batista dictatorship.

began to fall apart. Alemán had absolute control over the money and was supplying all the resources for the expedition; but meanwhile Trujillo bought Genovevo Pérez, the head of the army, and that is when the conflicts between all the groups calling themselves revolutionary came to the surface. Many believed that they were revolutionary. They truly believed it, because what was a revolution? They did not know. Who could be the flag bearers of a revolution or express revolutionary ideas? The communists, those who were defending the workers, those with an ideology, a revolutionary theory? Many considered that the revolution meant punishing the thugs from the Machado era or the Batista era who had committed crimes against the people. That was their idea of being a revolutionary.

Everything began to deteriorate. It was also the time of the Orfila massacre. This group, which had the full weight of the police, repressive forces and all the rest behind them, were in a family home and shooting broke out. In their attempt to capture and kill one of the leaders of opposition groups, they killed even the lady of the house along with everyone else. The army was sent in and the battle lasted four hours. This occurred while we were in Cayo Confites.

A journalist who managed to take photos of the whole thing became famous; it was a huge scandal. Genovevo, the head of the army, took advantage of the incident to call off the Dominican expedition, which quite logically he saw would boost his domestic political rival if the rebel movement in the Dominican Republic was successful. So they took advantage of the situation to wipe out any possible rivals. They imprisoned many of the top men, took away their power in the motorcycle police force, the Bureau of Enemy Activities, the judiciary, the secret and national police. They were removed from all the high places; they lost all their power.

Guerrilla warfare

So when the Dominican invasion was frustrated — while we were on our way to the Dominican Republic — there was widespread desertion. From that moment on I had the idea of guerrilla warfare. I had been given a company of soldiers. The whole thing was totally chaotic: no organization, no efficiency, no nothing. But I said to myself, we have to go. I almost started guerrilla warfare in the Dominican Republic; on the basis of Cuban experiences and my conviction that one could fight against the army, I was already thinking of the possibility of a guerrilla war in the mountains of the Dominican Republic. That was in 1947.

On my return I was not put in prison. I had not resigned myself to the idea of going to prison — that is also a long story. I managed to hold on to some weapons, which were later lost because of a betrayal. Just when everyone in Havana thought that I had been swallowed up by the sharks of Nipe Bay, the dead man turned up on the steps of the university. No one could believe their eyes, because I had not made contact with anyone until I arrived in Havana.

The battle of Orfila had brought about a change in the situation. The intervention of the army, the disarming of the main group that dominated the university, had brought about optimal conditions and I think it can be said that the support of the students was total.

I was then faced with the following problem: the expedition was around June or July and had been extended beyond September. I was supposed to take exams in certain subjects in September. But by the time I arrived, exam time was already over and I was faced with a choice — to enroll for the second year again as an official student, in order to continue with my work within the official institutions of the FEU, or to simply enroll for examinations. That was a very important decision, because I could never tolerate eternal students and eternal leaders who enrolled time and time again. I had strongly criticized this and could not do the same myself. So I simply enrolled for examinations only.

Then I was faced with the contradiction of having many, very many supporters at the university but I was not able to run for official posts within the organization. But I did not hesitate in making that decision, and I am satisfied with what I did at that time.

When I returned, the situation had improved considerably; it was safer and calmer. That was when I took on the task of trying to organize a Latin American students' conference in Colombia, which would coincide with the famous OAS meeting,[15] where they were going to pass I don't know how many reactionary resolutions. We managed to get some people together. I visited Venezuela and Panama, places of considerable activity. While I was working with

[15] The Organization of American States (OAS) was established at a meeting in Bogotá, Colombia, March 30–May 2, 1948. It became a means of U.S. control of Latin America and of opposition to revolutionary Cuba, as well as the Soviet Union.

the students in Colombia, I was put in touch with Gaitán, a leader of exceptional talent with great popular support, who unfortunately was assassinated on that April 9, just one hour before he was to meet with us for the second time. We were preparing to meet with him when the insurrection broke out in Bogotá.[16]

Revolutionary consciousness

The most important thing for me was my political training and developing a revolutionary consciousness. I had traditional ideas concerning the War of Independence and [José] Martí's writings; I strongly supported Martí and his thinking. I had read virtually everything there was to read on the wars of independence; then I became acquainted with economic concepts and the absurdities of capitalism and developed my own utopian way of thinking — a utopian socialism, rather than scientific socialism. I was concerned with the chaotic nature of things, how everything is disorganized, with excessive affluence in some places and unemployment in others; an overabundance of food in some places and hunger in others. I was becoming aware of the chaotic nature of capitalist society and was coming to the conclusion that that type of economy, which they taught us about, was absurd.

That is why, when I first came across Marx's famous *Communist Manifesto*, it had a great impact on me. I was also aided by certain university texts, such as *La historia de la legislación obrera* [*History of Labor Legislation*], written by someone who later was not faithful to that history; also the work of Raúl Roa[17] and other political books. In other words, I was able to refine my ideas with the help of texts written by various professors. I was also aided by the Popular Socialist Party[18] bookstore, where I bought everything on credit because I never had sufficient funds to pay outright. As a result, I gradually built up a complete Marxist-Leninist library of my own. It

---

[16] See next chapter for a more detailed account of Fidel Castro's participation in the Bogotá uprising.

[17] Raúl Roa (1907–82) was exiled in the 1930s and helped found the Anti-Imperialist Cuban Revolutionary Organization. In 1940 he became assistant dean of the faculty of Social Sciences at the University of Havana; he was to later serve as dean until 1963. After the 1959 revolution, he became Cuba's ambassador to the Organization of American States and for over a decade was minister for foreign relations.

[18] Popular Socialist Party was Cuba's communist party.

was my professors who provided me with the materials which I later began to read avidly.

The Orthodox Party was founded around that time, and I joined right from the beginning. Later I became a socialist and something like the left wing of the Orthodox Party.

So what was the key element in this? My conviction was that the Communist Party was isolated, and due to the prevailing conditions at the height of the Cold War and the vast amount of anticommunist prejudice at the time in Cuba, it was not possible to make a revolution based on the policies of the Popular Socialist Party, even though it wanted to make a revolution. The United States and the reactionaries within Cuba had isolated this party sufficiently to prevent it absolutely from carrying out a revolution. That's when I began to think about other possible ways and means of carrying out a revolution.

Given the level of activity in the country at the time and the great popularity of Chibás' movement among the masses, I saw myself as being part of a party with broad popular support, attractive concepts in the struggle against vice and political corruption, and social ideas that were not yet quite revolutionary. Except in Havana, generally the party was falling into the hands of large landowners. Whenever a popular party emerged, the provincial administrations soon fell into the hands of the landowners and the wealthy. It was the same in the Orthodox Party. Due to this contradiction and the tragic death of its strong and militant founder, I formulated the concept of how a revolution should take place in Cuba's conditions.

With Chibás' suicide,[19] that party was left without a leader. We needed to win the elections. As a result of the support gained after the death of Chibás, it was inevitable that the Orthodox Cuban People's Party won the elections.

Faced with the impossibility of a revolution and the inevitability of it being rapidly thwarted, I prepared a plan for the future: to launch a revolutionary program and organize a people's uprising from within that government and from within Congress itself. From that time on, I already had the concept totally worked out. I had established all the ideas that are in *La historia me absolverá* [*History*

---

[19] Orthodox Party leader Eduardo Chibás publicly committed suicide in 1951 to protest against government corruption.

will absolve me],[20] the measures that were required and how to institute them. That was the first revolutionary strategy that I was able to draw up, barely six years after having started university. One could say that it took me six years to acquire a revolutionary consciousness and draw up a revolutionary strategy.

July 26 Movement is launched

All of that changed when the March 10 [1952] coup occurred,[21] since it cut short that process and established a military government by force. That was another challenge and it was not our plan to make the revolution on our own. We thought that an elemental sense of national interest — an elemental sense of patriotic honor — would cause the opposition forces to come together to fight Batista. We began to prepare for that time, to fight alongside the other forces in what we believed was an inevitable and essential event for our country; we began to prepare the people here in the university. It was a secret operation; some 1,200 members of the July 26 Movement were trained in the University Martyrs' Room here.

My experience in Cayo Confites and the problems with the expedition had taught me a lot. Our experiences during the first months of the clandestine struggle taught us a great deal about how to work, and we came to train some 1,200 members before July 26, with the cooperation of a number of comrades from the FEU and the university.

I'm going to explain something else which I have never done before — I had to train the people of the July 26 Movement secretly in the university, because there was a great deal of jealousy among the students following the March 10 coup. There were people who believed that history would repeat itself and the university would take the lead again, as it had in 1933. In fact, this is what happened, but it came about in another way. And so, I have to say with great bitterness that there was jealousy among some of the students. So I had to work clandestinely.

---

[20] *History will absolve me* was Fidel Castro's defense speech at his secret trial on October 16, 1953, after the July 26 attack on the Moncada garrison. The speech was later smuggled out of the prison on the Isle of Pines and published as a pamphlet, which became the basic program of the revolutionary struggle, known as the Moncada Program.
[21] On March 10, 1952, Batista staged a coup, suspended the Constitution and became dictator of Cuba.

When the March 10 coup took place, the only people who had money, millions, resources of all kinds, were the members of the overthrown government; and they began to mobilize their resources to buy arms. Of course, those people felt a great deal of hatred toward me. You only have to look at the charges I made in the *Alerta* newspaper in the weeks leading up to the March 10 coup, which were given the prominence of the front page headlines in the paper with the largest circulation in the country at that time. That was in January, February of that year [1952]. They tried to blame me for the coup d'état, even before I wrote two other articles, which were stronger still, bearing the rallying cry: "You don't have to go to Guatemala."

This all stemmed from the fact that Chibás committed suicide, accusing several politicians of having estates in Guatemala, but he could not prove it. He was subjected to extraordinary pressure; he became desperate and killed himself. I wrote that you did not have to go to Guatemala, and I revealed all the property that those people had here and all of the dirty deals that they were involved in. My new profession as a lawyer came to good use to access the property registries and all the title deeds; all these documents were presented as irrefutable proof and caused a great impact.

Thus, those people sought to blame me for the demoralization, which had led to the coup d'état — a senseless, unfounded idea but a strong one. I found myself facing tremendous hatred on one side, and jealousy in the university. But no one should be left uncertain, there was never any hatred or jealousy on the part of José Antonio Echevarría,[22] never; he was always a good comrade and a good friend. However, the problem was that there were people who wanted to wrench the revolution away from the university. Those were the conditions in which we organized the July 26 Movement. When we saw the enormous errors of those who could have assisted the rebellion with all their resources, the divisions between parties and organizations and the incapacity for action, we realized that there was no alternative; we decided to initiate the armed struggle with the

---

[22] José Antonio Echevarría, was the leader of the Revolutionary Directorate, which signed a pact with the July 26 Movement in September 1956 in Mexico, unifying Cuban youth and the revolutionary forces against the Batista dictatorship. He was killed in an assault on the Presidential Palace in Havana in March 1957 at the age of 24.

forces of the July 26 Movement.

I believe that in any analysis of my life, nothing was more valuable for me than those years of struggle in the university.

We continued to be united to the university in all the preparations for July 26. We took part in those demonstrations because we had the strength. There were many organizations and there were a great many people involved in one or another of those organizations. We succeeded in forming an organization of 1,200 trained members.

We used many legal channels, including the district office of the Orthodox Party at 109 Prado [in Havana]. I met there with each one of the cells. We sent them to train in the university and then to other places. It was an enormous task based fundamentally within the youth movement of the Orthodox Party, which, as I said, had great influence at a grassroots level. It had a significant following among the young people; some 90 percent of the comrades chosen came from the ranks of the youth movement of the Orthodox Party. We managed to carry out this recruitment working from below.

The revolution begins

We could only use around 160 of those people for the attack on the Moncada garrison; for each member we used at Moncada and in Bayamo, there were eight who could not take part. We were really able to make a good selection from the groups that had made it that far, but all in complete legality.

There are many stories and interesting anecdotes those months from March 10, 1952, until July 26, 1953. Suffice it to tell you one fact: I covered some 50,000 kilometers in a little car I had, a Chevrolet 50-315. I had bought it on credit; they were always taking it away from me. It burned out two days before the Moncada attack. However, at that time we rented cars. We were working in a different way, as you would expect, fitting to the conditions.

There was one thing in our favor: Batista's police did not pay us much attention, since they were watching the Authentic Party, the Triple A[23] and those people who had hundreds and thousands of weapons. They knew that we had no weapons and that we had no resources; it seemed like just a pastime. They did not attach much importance to us, and that helped us to work within the law all of

---

[23] Triple A was an underground organization led by Aureliano Sanchez, a former minister in the government of Carlos Prío, overthrown by Batista.

that time, apart from a few odd occasions in which we had to keep a low profile.

If there is something that I still need to say, it is that although there were conflicts here in this university, which I have mentioned, many of those who were our enemies here, and even some of those who wanted to kill me and were making plans to kill me, later joined the movement during the revolution, above all in the guerrilla war in the Sierra Maestra. So, many of those who were adversaries here, and strong adversaries at that, later joined the July 26 Movement to fight, and some of them died. So, you can see the paradoxes that are a part of life, and how certain times give way to others. They had confidence and they joined us. I've always had a great deal of admiration and respect for the comrades who did that.

When I came to university 50 years ago I found a fragmented society, a fragmented university, where the anti-imperialist spirit had been forgotten, where one could almost count the few communists there were on the fingers of one hand. We have such a different university here today.

In those days, there were enthusiastic young men and women; they rapidly mobilized for a demonstration. However, there was no political consciousness, there was no revolutionary consciousness. There was the restless, rebellious temperament of young people and there were the heroic traditions of the university. When I arrived at this university, I was very rapidly imbued with the university traditions, such as the events of November 27 and the execution of the students in 1871,[24] the death of Trejo, the death of Mella, the history of Mella, of Martínez Villena, the history of those who died, although they were not communists like Mella and Villena — all this history, back to the even more distant times of Céspedes and Ignacio Agramonte.[25]

That air of heroic tradition imbued the university and could be felt, and it had its effect on many people. The atmosphere of this university and the raw material we worked with had a special effect on us.

---

[24] On November 27, 1871, eight medical students were executed in Havana by the Spanish colonial regime.
[25] Carlos Manuel de Céspedes (1819–74) and Ignacio Agramonte (1841–73) were key figures in Cuba's struggle for independence against Spain.

I began by telling you what a bad student I was. Now, that was so, but I never got a grade I did not deserve; I never cribbed on certain questions; I studied all the subjects.

There is an academic record of the 47 subjects in which I was tested over a year or so. I enrolled for 20 without being an official student, and I sat down to study, in the midst of other activities, and I passed 20 subjects in a year. I enrolled for 30 the next. It wasn't that I had a mania for registering for classes. I had to do it, because I wanted to get four degrees: law, diplomatic law, administrative law and then a doctorate in social sciences and public law. I only had three subjects left for the latter, which I already knew very well.

At that time I was thinking of taking a break in order to study and I wanted to study political economy, but I needed a scholarship. I had to pass those 50 subjects to get the scholarship, and I had managed it. However, at that time events in Cuba gathered momentum and I changed my plans. I gave up on those projects and devoted myself entirely to the revolutionary struggle.

Don't take me as a role model. I don't consider myself to be a role model, much less a model of a good student. I have tried to be a good revolutionary. I have tried to be a good soldier. And if it does occur to some of you to imitate a case like mine, I beg you to imitate my few successes and spare yourselves the many errors that I may have committed.

And so, with absolute, total and sincere modesty, I accept the affection with which you have honored me this night, and the obligation to take on that horrible task of having to talk about myself.

3

Colombia 1948:
A Taste of Revolution

I was at the university and had nearly finished my third year of law. At the end of the school year in 1947, the Dominican revolutionaries, who had been struggling for many years, organized an expedition to the Dominican Republic. At that time, a member of the Cuban Government gave them some assistance in organizing their expedition. I don't want to tell you about that expedition and the mistakes its organizers made, because that's another topic, but the thing is I was president of the law school — a university student official.

Expedition to the Dominican Republic
At that time, in 1947, I was finishing my third year in my major, and I still had some exams to take. I was president of the law school, although this was under dispute. Associates of the Grau Administration controlled the university; a majority of the law school delegates had removed the president, who was very closely associated with the government, and had elected me instead. The

---

*In September 1981, Colombian journalist Arturo Alape interviewed Fidel Castro about his youthful exploits as an international student activist and his participation in and organization of solidarity actions with the popular movements in the Dominican Republic, Panama, Puerto Rico and Colombia. This interview, which has been slightly abridged, is published here for the first time in English.

government-controlled university authorities did not want to recognize me. So, officially, I was vice-president of the school and had also just been elected Chairman of the Committee for Dominican Democracy (CPDD) at the University of Havana.

The expedition to the Dominican Republic was organized in July, near the end of the school year. I thought that because of my contacts with the exiled Dominican leaders — especially Rodríguez, their main leader at the time — my first dutywas to sign up as a rank-and-file soldier, even though I hadn't helped to organize the expedition. And that's what I did. (I hadn't had anything to do with organizing the expedition because the government and governmental figures had taken charge of this, and I was opposed to the government. The organizers had resources both from Dominicans and from the government.)

There were around 1,200 men in the expedition. It was very badly organized; there were good people, many good Dominicans and Cubans who truly supported the Dominican cause, but also — as a result of too hasty recruiting — delinquents, some lumpen elements and all kinds of others.

I joined that expedition as a rank-and-file soldier. We spent several months training on Cayo Confites.[1] I was given the rank of lieutenant in command of a platoon. In the end, events took place in Cuba that caused conflict between the civilian government and the army, and the army decided to call off the expedition. In this dangerous situation, some of the men deserted, and I was placed in command of a company in one of the battalions of expeditionaries.

Then we left for the Dominican Republic. However, around 24 hours before we would have arrived, when we were still in the Bay of Nipe, we were intercepted and everybody was arrested — everybody but me, because I escaped by sea. More than anything else, it was a matter of honor for me not to be arrested. I was ashamed that the members of the expedition should wind up arrested, so I threw myself into the water, swam to Cayo Saitía and got away.

Meanwhile, August, September and October [1947] had been spent training for the expedition, and I lost the chance to take my examinations. That meant that I lost my rights as a student official at the university unless I enrolled in third year again. I hated those student officials who did not pass courses, and became eternal student

---

[1] A key located in northern Cuba.

leaders. So I did not enroll officially but studied on my own the third-year courses I still had to pass and the fourth-year ones as well. Although, I had no political rights as an official, I did have a lot of influence among the university students because of my opposition to the Grau regime. At one time, without intending to do so, I became the focal point of the struggle against the Grau Administration. That was in 1948.

Support for anti-imperialist movements

At around that time, I also participated in the Puerto Rican struggle; because I had contact with Albizu Campos and his family and other Puerto Rican leaders, I had become an activist for Puerto Rican independence. In summary, I was chairman of the Committee for Dominican Democracy and had taken part in the expedition (even though it didn't get anywhere); and I also played an active part in the struggle for Puerto Rican independence, as well as participating in political activities in Cuba, which mainly consisted of criticizing and protesting against the corrupt government.

At that time I also supported other Latin American causes, such as the demand that the Panama Canal be returned to Panama. It was an era of student agitation in Panama — and also in Venezuela, because the dictatorship had been overthrown, and Rómulo Gallegos had just been elected president of Venezuela. Moreover, sharp conflicts already existed between [Argentina's Juan] Perón[2] and the United States.

Therefore, I was active in those movements and generally supported the end of colonialism in Latin America. Those were the four main points, which led me to establish some contacts — tactical ones — with the Peronists, who were not only struggling against the United States but were also claiming the Malvinas Islands, which were an English colony. The Peronists carried out actions, sent delegations to different countries, met with students and distributed materials. This was a tactical arrangement.

The Organization of American States [OAS][3] was going to hold a

---

[2] Juan Perón was president of Argentina 1946–55 and from 1973 until his death in 1974.
[3] The Organization of American States (OAS) was formed at a meeting in Bogotá, Colombia, March 30–May 2, 1948, with the support of the Truman Administration. The Charter of the OAS went into effect in December 1951, and later became a means of U.S. control of Latin America and of opposition to

meeting in 1948, sponsored by the United States, to consolidate its dominance in Latin America. It occurred to me to hold a meeting of Latin American students at the same time and in the same place as the OAS meeting, to uphold anti-imperialist principles and support the struggles against dictatorships in Latin America, not only the Dominican Republic, but also other Latin American countries struggling for democracy.

It was my idea to hold the congress, so I began to make contacts with the Panamanian students, who were very active in the struggle for the Canal's return, and also with the Venezuelans. I knew about the situation in various countries. I thought that my first stop would be Venezuela, where a revolution had just taken place and the students had a very revolutionary attitude; then I would visit Panama and Colombia. I was going to present the idea to students at those universities and ask for their cooperation. At the same time, the Argentines also cooperated and pledged to mobilize the students in their country. Of course, I paid my own way. I had very little money — just enough for my ticket.

Alape: Did a delegation of Peronists arrive in Cuba at that time?

Castro: I had made contact with a delegation of young Peronists who were in Cuba then. We coordinated things so they would work in certain areas, and I would work in others. In this way, the Latin American leftists organized the Latin American students' congress. I acted as the representative of the Cuban students, even though I had some conflicts with the official leadership of the Cuban Federation of University Students [FEU], some of whom had relations with the government. In other words, I was not an official representative of the FEU, but I did represent the vast majority of the students, who supported me and considered me their leader, even though I could not be an FEU official at that time.

Organizing Latin American students

So, I left for Venezuela. The planes back then kept hopping from one place to another. I remember that the first thing that occurred to me was that the plane might land in the Dominican Republic. When it did, I did a stupid thing and got off the plane. I thought somebody had recognized me, and I started talking with some people in the Dominican airport. But I was lucky, and the stopover was a short

revolutionary Cuba, as well as the Soviet Union.

one. Soon I got back on the plane. Nothing had happened.

There was a heated atmosphere in Venezuela. I visited the offices of the governmental newspaper — the one put out by the party in power. I made contacts with the Venezuelan students; I presented the idea of the congress, and they liked it.

I met with students of the Central University, who at that time were members of Democratic Action. I asked them to support the organization of the congress and invited them to participate. The Venezuelan students liked the idea and decided to send a delegation to the congress. I asked for an interview with Rómulo Gallegos who had recently been elected president to set forth my ideas. I went to La Guaira to meet with Rómulo Gallegos and I asked him also to support the congress.

Alape: Why did you want to talk with Rómulo Gallegos?

Castro: Because Rómulo Gallegos had a lot of prestige. He was both a political and a literary figure. The Venezuelan revolution had had a big impact in Cuba and had inspired a lot of support. Moreover, most of the students belonged to Gallegos's party. So my interest in paying my respects to him was related to the fact that he was the leader of a country that had made a democratic revolution and a figure with international prestige. I was asking for the Venezuelan students' support for the congress we were going to hold, although I had already obtained that support; so it was also a matter of courtesy, of getting to know him and of telling him about it.

After that, I flew to Panama — now with the support of the revolutionary Venezuelan students. I met with the student leaders in Panama. There had just been shooting during the protests against the U.S. occupation of the Canal, and a Panamanian student had been wounded and permanently maimed. He became a symbol for all the other students. I made contacts and visited him. The Panamanian students were very worked up and very strongly in favor of the idea of the congress. They decided to send a delegation to Bogotá. So now two important countries were in favor.

From Panama, I flew to Bogotá. I did not have much money left, just enough to get a room at a hotel. I did not know what I was going to do after that, so I went to a small two- or three-story hotel, which was very pleasant. In those days, everything was very cheap, and if you brought dollars into the country — I had a few — the exchange rate was very favorable; food and lodging at a hotel didn't cost very much. As soon as I signed into the hotel, I made contact with the university students. The vast majority of the students were leftist Liberals. [Liberal leader] Gaitán had a lot of prestige and influence in the university.

Alape: The official investigation of the April 9 uprising mentions a communist plot. There is even a document published in Colombia that Blas Roca[4] was supposed to have written, giving instructions to the Colombian Communists. Every year, when articles are published about that date, documents appear saying that you were a tool of international Communism. Were you a communist at that time?

Castro: I had already read some Marxist literature; I had studied political economy, for example, and had some knowledge of political theory. I was attracted by the basic ideas of Marxism, and I had acquired a socialist awareness throughout my university studies, as I came into contact with Marxist literature. At that time, there were a few Communist students in the University of Havana; I had friendly relations with them, but I was not a member of the Communist Youth or the Communist Party. My activities had nothing at all to do with the Communist Party of that era. At that time, I had an anti-imperialist awareness. I had friendly relations with several young Communists, who were good activists and very stoical, whom I liked and admired. But neither the Communist Party of Cuba nor the Communist Youth had anything to do with the organization of the Bogotá congress. In that period, I was acquiring a revolutionary awareness; I had initiative, I was active, but I was an independent fighter.

Alape: What were the first contacts you made?

Castro: Wherever I went, the first thing I did was go to the university students. I immediately looked for the university leaders, met with them and presented the idea of the congress. They agreed with it completely. That is, the Venezuelan, Panamanian and Colombian students liked the idea of the congress and welcomed it with a lot of enthusiasm, and all of them contacted other Latin American student organizations. We had made some contacts, and

---

[4] Blas Roca (1908–87) was the general secretary of the Communist Party of Cuba (later known as the Popular Socialist Party and the Communist Revolutionary Union) from 1934 until 1961 when the party fused with the July 26 Movement and the Revolutionary Directorate to become the Integrated Revolutionary Organizations.

the Argentines had made others — I'm not going to say that all the students were represented, because no Latin American congresses had ever been held before — but it was a very representative group. We thought that the students should be organized and take an active part in the struggle for the anti-imperialist cause. I thought there should be an organization, and I even had the idea of creating an organization of Latin American students. I took all those steps, and the congress was organized.

Alape: Did you make contact with the Guatemalan students, who were a very interesting political phenomenon at that time?

Castro: I can't remember in detail, but, even though the congress was organized in a very short time, there were representatives of the various progressive, leftist forces in Latin America.

An interesting situation arose: I was the organizer of the congress, and everybody accepted the role I was playing; but when the official leaders of the Cuban FEU saw that the congress was a reality, they wanted to take part officially and sent representatives, who included Alfredo Guevara, then secretary of the organization, and [Enrique Ovares,] the president of the FEU. When they arrived, the question of representation arose in one of the first meetings: whether or not I could represent the Cuban university students. The issue was discussed in a plenary session; I spoke quite vehemently, explaining everything I had done, how I'd done it and why. The students supported me almost unanimously following my presentation, which was rather impassioned, as was only to be expected given my age at the time. In fact, I presided over that meeting. In my speech I said that I had no personal interest, that I was not after personal honors of any kind, that my only interest was the congress. I said that I was willing to give up all positions and honors, and that I only wanted the struggle and the congress to take place. The students applauded and supported the proposal that I continue as organizer of the congress.

Impressions of Bogotá

I think I must have arrived around five or six days before April 9, the day of the uprising. I can't remember everything I did in Bogotá, but I do remember how impressed I was with that city. It was the first time in my life that I had been in Bogotá or anywhere else in Colombia, and the city was very different from anything I had ever known before. About half the streets were avenues, and the first thing

I had to do was understand that the avenues went in one direction, and the streets in the other.

I was also struck by the large number of people in the streets all day long, especially on 7th Avenue, which was near my hotel. I also could not understand, neither then or now, why so many people in the streets were wearing overcoats. Perhaps it was colder back then than it is now. The city hadn't grown so much. It wasn't a modern city; it was quite old. There were many cafés; it seems that there was a Colombian custom of going to the cafés to drink coffee, beer or soft drinks — and everybody wore overcoats. For me, it was a very curious thing to always see a large number of people in the streets. Maybe there was large-scale unemployment, but, even so, I can't understand why there were so many people on the streets of Bogotá at all hours of the day and night.

Naturally, with the OAS meeting being held there, the city was prepared and a special police force had been created to handle the conference. Its members had been given bright new uniforms.

I made my contacts rapidly, calling the first few meetings for organizing the congress, which was to conclude with a meeting in the stadium that was used for mass rallies — a stadium or a large square, I don't remember which.

Right away, the students talked to me about Gaitán. At that time, Gaitán was the most prestigious political figure, the one with the greatest popular support. Without any doubt, he was considered the person who would win the next election in Colombia. The vast majority of the students supported Gaitán. I had no contact with the Colombian Communist Party, though the people I met with at the university included some Liberals and Communists. Liberals and other leftists had taken up the idea of the congress with enthusiasm and were working to organize it. The Liberal students placed me in contact with Gaitán and took me to visit him.

Alape: According to my information, that was on April 7. Is that right?

Castro: It must have been April 7, because we went to tell Gaitán about our ideas and to ask for his support. Gaitán was enthusiastic about the proposal for the congress and offered to support it. He talked with us, and he agreed that the congress should conclude with a mass meeting. He promised that he would give the closing address. Naturally, we were very pleased and very optimistic about Gaitán's support and his promise to participate, because it guaranteed the success of the congress. He told us to come back to his office — I think it was on 7th Avenue — two days later at 2:00 or 2:15 p.m. on the afternoon of April 9.

On this occasion, he gave me some political materials and explained the situation in Colombia. He also gave me a pamphlet with his famous speech known as the "Prayer for Peace," which was a magnificent piece of oratory.

There was a lot of agitation in Colombia at that time. Every day, there were 20 or 30 murders; every day, the newspapers had banner headlines saying that 30 farmers had been murdered in one place and another 25 farmers had been murdered somewhere else. While I was there, the newspapers carried accounts of such political assassinations practically every day. The papers also explained Gaitán's role; his struggle to find a solution to the violence; the March of Silence he had organized had been an impressive demonstration, with tens — or hundreds — of thousands of people marching in absolute silence, at the end of which he delivered his "Prayer for Peace." I immediately set about reading all those materials and absorbing Colombia's situation.

A very famous trial was held at that time — the trial of Lieutenant Cortés. I think there had been an incident between a military man and a journalist, which led to the death of the latter. This trial was just ending. I knew about Gaitán's role as a political figure and his political ideas from the students I met. He was also known as an exceptional lawyer and I was invited to attend the last session of the trial, in which Gaitán was defending Lieutenant Cortés; so I went. The trial was being broadcast over the radio, and practically everybody — even soldiers in the garrisons — listened to Gaitán's defense speech. At that time, the trial had become an important political issue. Since I was a law student, I listened with special interest, and I remember some parts, such as those in which he spoke of the bullet's trajectory, and mentioned some treatises of anatomy, including some French treatises that were famous in the schools of medicine. As a law student, I was very interested in the case and in the statement and the truly brilliant summing-up he made.

So while I was in Colombia, apart from the violence and bloodshed, a trial was taking place that was becoming very important politically. People in the army, the police stations and the garrisons listened to Gaitán's summing-up with interest; not only the military, but also public opinion was favorable to Lieutenant Cortés. Gaitan was very prominent and popular at that time.

Alape: A committee of military men had raised money to get Gaitán to defend him. What did you think of Gaitán during your meeting about the congress and later, as a lawyer?

Castro: Gaitán impressed me very favorably. First of all, I was influenced by the opinions of the majority of the people and the admiration expressed by the students with whom I had met. Then I had a talk with him. He appeared of Indian descent, wise and very intelligent. I had his speeches, especially the "Prayer for Peace," which was really the address of a virtuoso, an eloquent speaker who was a veritable master of the language. I was impressed by him because he identified with the most progressive position of the country, against the Conservative government. I was also impressed as a lawyer, because he was a brilliant politician, a brilliant orator and a brilliant lawyer.

All those things made a great impression on me; I also liked the interest he had taken in our ideas about the students' congress and the ease, willingness and generosity with which he supported us. He promised to help us and to appear at the mass meeting that would conclude the congress, which undeniably showed that he agreed with our views and was against the farce of the OAS meeting. All of those factors made me feel very friendly toward him. I also saw clearly that the vast majority of the people supported him.

Arrest in Bogotá

Something else happened during the days I was in Bogotá, busy in student meetings, organizing the congress and meeting with Gaitán. A gala performance was held in a theater in the city — I don't remember its name, but it was a very beautiful theater in the classical style. I think the gala had something to do with the governmental delegations that were taking part in the OAS conference. Since we were young and still rather immature, we had some pamphlets printed setting forth the slogans of the congress: the struggle for democracy in the Dominican Republic, the struggle for Puerto Rican independence, the return of the Panama Canal, an end to colonialism in Latin America, the return of the Malvinas Islands to Argentina and the struggle for democracy. We took the pamphlets to the theater and distributed them there. Technically, we may have been breaking the law — I don't know — but we didn't do it with that intention; we simply wanted to publicize our congress. Later, we were arrested. It seems that, soon after I got there, the secret police learned that some students were organizing a congress and learned about our activities. So it was not just our distributing the pamphlets at the theater — which seemed the most natural thing in the world to me, as we often did that in Cuba — but, as a result of that, the police arrested us. I don't remember exactly where I was or how they arrested me, but I think it was at the hotel.

Alape: The report says that they arrested you at the theater and then took you to Immigration.

Castro: You may be right. The fact is that they came for us, arrested us and took us to a gloomy office. It was on a side street, a place with dark passageways; they took us there with the pamphlets. But I think they arrested me at the hotel, or at least I'm sure they searched my room at the hotel later on. The records may clear this up. I know that we were taken along some side streets to some dirty buildings.

Alape: Who was arrested?

Castro: I was, and the other Cuban who was with me — there were two of us — and perhaps a Colombian student. I don't remember exactly. They took us into that building with the passageways, sat us down and questioned us. Perhaps out of idealism, in the ardor of youth, we told the authorities who we were and what we were doing — all about the congress, what our goals were in the congress, about Puerto Rico and the Panama Canal, what was in the pamphlet and the ideas with which we were organizing the congress. We were rather lucky in our talk with the detectives. In fact, I got the impression that somebody in charge even liked what we were saying. We were quite persuasive. They may have realized that we were far from dangerous and that we weren't sticking our noses into the country's internal problems. After the interrogation, they opened dossiers on us and let us go. They may have done this because they liked some of the things we were saying; I don't know. We may have been running a bigger risk than we imagined, but we weren't aware of it then. After the interrogation, we went back to the hotel and calmly resumed our activities.

Alape: But they followed you...

Castro: They probably did, but, in any case, we weren't doing anything illegal. All we were doing was organizing a students' congress, and we were in contact with one of the most important political figures in the country. They probably did not think much of those activities. In fact, objectively, apart from the ideological question and the goals we sought, we represented no danger for the Colombian Government. What we were doing had nothing to do with Colombia's internal problems; we were defending a Latin American idea. The only thing that might have bothered them was the fact that I met with students and with Gaitán. Apart from that, we were handing out pamphlets, which isn't a criminal offense anywhere in the world except under a repressive government. We had very naively handed out our pamphlets at the theater, with no desire to cause trouble. We were opposing the United States, not the Colombian Government.

We kept on with our activities, even though they were following us. I imagine that one of the tasks of detectives is to follow people. I did not realize that anybody was following me, because I was not engaged in any subversive activities against Colombia. All my energies went into working on the students' congress. There's no reason for me to claim any merit I don't deserve; there's no reason for me to portray myself as a subversive or as anybody important. I had my ideas and goals, and I was busy with the idea of the congress and the organization of the Latin American students. I had absolutely nothing against Colombia, apart from being horrified by all the massacres that were reported in the newspapers, and I liked Gaitán. That is what I remember most about those days prior to April 9.

Alape: Did you have a meeting with the local CTC trade union?

Castro: In the beginning stages, we had several activities: a meeting with the university students; a meeting with the first delegates from several places, in which the issue of representation was raised; and a meeting with workers. The Colombians made those contacts and organized the meetings, but it was all related to the students' congress. There was nothing else. After the sensational events that occurred, it is possible that I may have forgotten some of the details.

April 9 uprising in Colombia

Alape: On April 11, the Colombian Government spoke of your stay in Bogotá, saying that you were near the place where Gaitán fell at 1:00 in the afternoon. That statement was based on the report made by the police who followed you. The government's accusation that you were linked with the April 9 uprising was based on that statement.

Castro: We had a meeting with Gaitán scheduled for 2:00 or 2:15 in the afternoon, to continue talking about the congress and get down to details about the mass meeting with which it was going to conclude, a meeting in which he was going to participate.

That day I had lunch at the hotel and was killing time, waiting for the appointment with Gaitán.

A few minutes after I left the hotel, people started running frantically in various directions. They looked crazy, running first in one direction and then another. I can assure you that nobody organized the April 9 uprising. I'm telling you this because I saw it almost from the start. I saw that April 9 was a completely spontaneous outbreak; nobody could have organized it. Only those who organized Gaitán's murder could have imagined what might occur. Those who organized the murder may have done so to eliminate a political adversary. They may have imagined the explosive reaction, but perhaps not even they could imagine it.

The fact is that, as soon as Gaitán was murdered, there was a tremendous explosive reaction of an entirely spontaneous nature. The thing that the April 9 uprising lacked was precisely organization. That is the key; it completely lacked organization.

It was around 1:20 when I left the hotel to walk around a little until the time of the appointment set for 2:00 or 2:15 that afternoon. Walking towards Gaitán's office I saw people running around desperately in all directions shouting, "They've killed Gaitán! They've killed Gaitán! They've killed Gaitán!" The people were angry and indignant, reflecting the tragic situation.

Significance of Gaitán's assassination

Alape: Speaking historically, why do you think Gaitán was killed?

Castro: I can't make any absolute statements about that. For example, the CIA could have killed Gaitán. Imperialism could have killed Gaitán, because he was the exponent of a progressive movement, a people's movement, which could not have been at all pleasing to imperialism. It is a logical theory.

The oligarchy could have killed Gaitán, and this is the most probable explanation. The Colombian oligarchy was involved in a struggle against the people, a power struggle, a struggle in which

Gaitán stood out as a candidate of the democratic forces in the country who was sure to be victorious. Unquestionably, Gaitán had a lot of prestige among the people. He had gained it gradually and was very popular; he had great personal magnetism; he was a leftist, anti-oligarchic political leader.

There was practically a civil war in Colombia at the time. If you look through the newspapers from that period, you can see that they speak of 20, 30, 40 or 70 dead nearly every day. While I was there, I was amazed by those massacres. Gaitán had united the Liberal Party and was sure to be the winning candidate in the coming election.

A madman could have killed Gaitán; it's possible. Whoever killed Gaitán was not taken prisoner, was not arrested. I think the crowd tore him apart; no confession was ever obtained from that man. I imagine that the Conservative authorities weren't all that interested in clearing things up, because the Conservative government could have done so. Who was that man? Where did he live? What links did he have? What group or party did he belong to?

The United States may have considered Gaitán a communist, even though, ideologically, he was no such thing. Gaitán was popular, democratic, progressive — above all, a great leader of the people.

I am sure that Gaitán would have had a great influence on Colombian politics. After his death, the oligarchy remained in power for many years. It still holds power. I think that Gaitán was a revolutionary — not a communist revolutionary, but a revolutionary nonetheless.

A spontaneous uprising

When I had walked around two more blocks I came to a tiny park, where people were carrying out acts of violence. Close to Gaitán's office, I kept walking along 7th Avenue and saw that people had already broken into some offices. I remember one incident: I saw a man in the park trying to break a typewriter that he had taken from somewhere. He was determined to break that typewriter, but he was having a terrible time trying to do it with his hands. So I said, "Give it to me," and I helped him. I took the machine and threw it up in the air and let it fall. When I saw that furious, desperate man, that was all I could think of.

As I kept on walking toward the park where Parliament was (and where the OAS conference was being held) I saw people breaking shop windows and other things. This began to worry me, because I already had some very clear, very precise ideas about what should and shouldn't happen in a revolution. I began to see expressions of anarchy there on 7th Avenue. I wondered what the leaders of the Liberal Party were doing and if anybody could control the situation.

By 1:30 or 1:45 p.m. I reached the corner of the square where Parliament is. Somebody was on a balcony to the left, speaking from the balcony. A few people were gathered there, expressing their anger with absolutely spontaneous violence. Several dozen people were in the park, shouting furiously, indignantly, and they began to break the park's lights, throwing stones at them, so you had to be careful, because the stones might hit you instead of the glass.

There was a line of very well-dressed, natty, well-organized policemen. As soon as the dozens or hundreds of people who were breaking the lights in the park and other things moved close to the door like a gust of wind, the cordon of police broke — as though they were demoralized — and all those people poured into the Palace.

I was in the middle of the park, with stones flying in all directions. They went into the Parliament building, which was around three or four stories high. I did not go in, but stayed just outside the building, watching that eruption — it was a veritable eruption of people. The people went up and started throwing chairs, desks and all kinds of things down from the upper floors. An avalanche of furniture came falling down. Meanwhile, a man was trying to give a speech from a balcony on a corner near the park, but nobody paid him any attention. It was an unbelievable scene.

I decided to go and see the two Cubans who did not live at the hotel: Enrique Ovares and Alfredo Guevara, a comrade of mine, who were staying in a rooming house not far from where I was. I went there to see what they thought of the situation and to tell them what I had seen. When I got to the rooming house, I talked with them for a few minutes, and then we saw an enormous procession of people — a river of people coming along a street that was more or less parallel to 7th Avenue. They had weapons; some had rifles, and others were armed with sticks or pieces of iron — everybody had a weapon of some kind. It was an enormous crowd — thousands of people — advancing along that street; it looked like a procession coming down that long, narrow street.

I didn't know where the crowd was going. Some said they were going to a divisional police headquarters, so I joined them. I got in the front line of that crowd, and we went to the divisional police headquarters. I realized that it was a revolution, so I decided to join it as one of its rank-and-file members. Naturally, I knew that the people were oppressed and were right to rebel; I also knew that Gaitán's death was a terrible crime. So I took sides. Up until then — until I saw the crowd coming by after I had visited the two Cubans — I hadn't done anything. But, when I saw the crowd on the move, I joined them. That was when I joined the rebelling crowd.

When we got to the [Third] Divisional Police headquarters, the police were dug in on the upper floor, aiming their rifles at us. Nobody knew what was going to happen. The crowd reached the entrance, which the police were keeping clear, but nobody fired.

Like an overflowing river, the crowd spread everywhere, getting weapons and other things. Some policemen had joined the crowd; you could see uniformed policemen in the crowd. The divisional headquarters was built around a central patio; the front part of the building was two stories high.

I don't know how many weapons there were; the few that were available had been taken from the policemen, though some policemen kept their weapons and joined the crowd. I went into the armory, but I didn't see any rifles — only some guns with long, thick tear-gas bullets. The only thing I could get my hands on was one of those tear-gas weapons. I began to fill a cartridge belt with those bullets, around 20 or 30 of them, and I told myself, "I don't have a rifle, but at least I have something to shoot" — a gun with a big barrel. I then realized, "Well, here I am in a suit and normal shoes; I'm not dressed for war." I found a cap without a visor and put it on, but I was still wearing my normal shoes, which were no good for fighting. Moreover, I wasn't very happy with my gun. I went out into the patio, which was full of people running everywhere — rushing up and down the stairs; civilians and police mixed up together. Some of the police had allowed themselves to be disarmed; others, who remained armed, had joined the crowd.

I ran up the stairs to the second floor and went into a room that turned out to be for the police officers. I was looking for something to wear and trying to see if there were any more weapons. I put on some boots, but they did not fit. An officer came in — I'll never forget this — and, in the midst of all that chaos, told me, "Not my boots, by god! Not my boots!" Since the boots did not fit me, I said,

"OK, mister; keep your boots."

I went down to the patio to join a squad or something, and I saw a police officer who was organizing one. I had no pretensions of being the chief of anything; I was a rank-and-file soldier. So I went there with my tear-gas gun and bullets and got in line. The officer, who had a rifle, looked at what I was carrying and said, "What are you doing with that?" I said, "It was the only thing I could find," and he asked for the gun. He did not seem too eager to fight, even though he was organizing a squad. He gave me his rifle and around 14 bullets. Of course, when he gave me the rifle, a whole lot of people tried to grab it, and I had to fight pretty hard to keep it. Well, I hung on to the rifle and the 14 bullets.

From then on, I had a rifle, but there was no organization. Just as they had swarmed in, crowds were going out, without knowing where they were going. Some people shouted that we should go to the Palace. I joined the crowd who said they were going somewhere — but nobody knew where. There was tremendous disorder, almost no discipline and no organization.

Our situation was difficult, because only two of the 12 or 14 of us had weapons. We decided to go and help the students who were at the National Broadcasting Station. The crowd had gone off in several directions when we heard the car with the loudspeaker saying that the National Broadcasting Station was being attacked, and we decided to go there. We did not know exactly where it was, but we wanted to go and help the students. We went to 7th Avenue and headed north, toward the Monserrate Hermitage.

On 7th Avenue, the crowd was attacking practically everything — stores and other buildings — and was beginning to loot, too. Some of the people were drinking; they came up with bottles of the medium-dark Colombian rum and said, "Hey, have a drink. Here!" Imagine: there I was with my rifle, and the other man with his rifle, and around 15 others without weapons, going up the avenue. There was a lot of confusion. Nobody knew what was happening. A lot of the police had rebelled, and people were saying that some military units had rebelled, too. At that moment, nobody knew what position the Colombian Army had taken. Unquestionably, Gaitán had had supporters among the military men, but there was a lot of confusion. We had to keep going and find people to ask the way [to the National Broadcasting Station].

A lot of offices and other places were on fire. We finally got to a place that I realized later was the Ministry of War. I remember that it had a park on the right and another on the left. When we got there, we saw a battalion of soldiers coming toward us, heading south. They had German-style helmets, which they wore back then, and rifles. A whole battalion and some tanks were advancing, but we did not know which side the army was on. So we took the precaution of moving about 20 meters away and ducking down behind some benches, waiting to see if the soldiers were friends or foes — remember, there were only around 12 of us, and we had only two rifles. They paid no attention to us and kept on marching down the street.

We crossed the street and went to the park that is in front of the Ministry of War. There was a door and some railings. I was filled with revolutionary fervor, trying to get as many people as possible to join the revolutionary movement, so I jumped up on a bench in front of the Ministry of War and harangued the military men who were there, trying to get them to join the revolution. Everybody heard me, nobody did anything. There I was with my rifle, giving my harangue on a bench. When I finished, I went on, because the students were leaving.

A bus that had been taken over by students was standing on the other side of the park, and I realized that it would take me toward the radio station. So, after I finished my harangue, I ran after the bus and caught it. The other armed comrade who was with me fell behind, and I did not see him again. I got on the bus with my rifle and the students who were going to help those in the National Broadcasting Station. I don't know how many blocks we went on the bus — maybe eight or 10. And, in the course of all this, I lost my wallet. It had only a few pesos in it, since I had practically no money, but somebody stole it.

We went toward the radio station and got off at a corner. It was an avenue, a kind of boulevard, on which the radio station fronted. We just flowed into the street. We now had only one rifle — mine — with which to support the students who were in the radio station. When we got to the avenue, there was a hell of a lot of shooting. As soon as we got there, they began to shoot at us with I don't know how many rifles. We managed to get down behind a bench and take cover, and miraculously they did not kill all of us. We managed to get to the corner again and followed a group of one man with a rifle and 10 or 12 others without weapons.

We could not do anything to free the students in the radio station, so we decided to go to the university to see if there was any organization, if the students had set up a command post or established some leadership.

Even by the time we got to the university, nothing had been organized. News came in about what was happening, and there were lots of people, none of whom had weapons. Not far from the university, there was a divisional police headquarters, which we decided to seize to obtain more weapons. I was the only one with a rifle, so it was assumed that I would have to seize it. A crowd of students and I headed for the headquarters.

It was suicidal. We were just lucky that when we got there we found that it had already been taken. The policemen had rebelled, and when we got there they welcomed us with open arms. The police and people were already fraternizing.

I presented myself to the head of the division, who happened to be the chief of all the police who had rebelled. I told him right away that I was a student and a Cuban and that I had come to attend a congress. I explained everything to him briefly, and he made me his aide. The police chief was a rather tall man; he was a major or colonel. So I became the aide of the police chief who had rebelled.

He decided to go to the Liberal Party's office. I got in a jeep with the police chief, and we went to the Liberal Party's headquarters. I was glad about this, because the disorganization and the chaos had worried me. I could not see any leadership or organization, so I was glad when I saw that the police chief was in contact with the Liberal Party. I thought that everything would begin to be organized.

When we got to the office, we walked up the stairs. I went with him up to the door. Then he went in, but I did not. I stayed outside. He went in and talked with the Liberal leaders who were there; I don't know who they were. Then we got back in the jeep and went back to the divisional headquarters near the university. There were two jeeps by then.

He stayed at the divisional headquarters where the police had rebelled for a while and then, because it was beginning to get dark, decided to go back to the Liberal Party's office. We went in two jeeps. He went in the first one, and I went in the second. All this time, both on the first trip and on this one, a lot of people accompanied us, because a group of unarmed students had stayed with me. This time, I stayed in the escort jeep outside the Liberal Party office, sitting in the front passenger seat.

An amazing thing happened shortly afterwards, and I did something Quixotic: it was already getting dark, and the first jeep, containing the police chief, had engine trouble and stopped. The driver could not start it again. The police chief and the passengers in the first jeep got out. I was disgusted. I got out of my jeep and told them, "You're all irresponsible." I gave my seat to the police chief, and I stayed in the middle of the street with two or three other students. I was on the sidewalk, standing by a long wall, alone, with no contacts. I was in a street next to the Ministry of War, as I learned later on. This was the second time I had bumped up against the Ministry of War.

After a few seconds, a small door in the wall opened, and, behind the small door, I saw an official cap and three or four men and several rifles with bayonets. I told the other students, "They're enemies. Let's cross the street." Taking advantage of the relative darkness, we crossed the street. I could not know for sure, but I suspected they were enemies when that little door opened and I saw an official cap and around four rifles with bayonets just six meters from us. In their uncertainty, they did not fire.

We walked down the street and I saw a man with a submachine gun. I could not tell whether he was a friend or foe, so I walked closer to him and asked who he was. He said, "I'm from the Fifth Police Division which has rebelled," so I found he was a friend.

That's when I decided to go to the Fifth Divisional Headquarters and join them. I had lost contact with the chief of police and decided to join what turned out to be the Fifth Division. By then, it was dark. Everything I've described took place between 1:30 and 6:30 p.m.

I went into the Fifth Divisional Headquarters and, as I did wherever I went, immediately identified myself: "I'm a Cuban student, participating in a congress." And, everywhere I went, I was immediately welcomed. So I went in. I did not have a cent, not even for a cup of coffee. There were a lot of policemen who had rebelled and some civilians — around 400 armed men — who were getting organized.

Alape: Did you meet Tito Orozco, the commander of that division?

Castro: Yes, I met him, the one who was acting as chief. There was a large patio in the middle, where the people were being organized, and as soon as I got there, I got in line and got organized along with them. Rather than setting up units, they were having an inspection, to see how many men there were. We were assigned to different places in the division's defense. I was told to go to the second floor. There was a dormitory there, and some policemen and I defended that floor. Every so often — every half hour, three quarters of an hour or hour, more or less — they had an inspection in the patio, and after that everybody went back to his post. The confusion continued, and nobody knew what was happening. This confusion lasted almost until the next day.

Meanwhile, what was going on in the streets? There were many people — they looked like ants — carrying loads. People were carrying refrigerators on their backs, or pianos. Unfortunately, because of the lack of organization, lack of training or the situation of extreme poverty or whatever, many of the people made off with everything they could find. Undeniably, there was looting; I saw it from the divisional headquarters. It worried me when I saw that instead of seeking a political solution for the situation, many people, without guidance, were looting.

Alape: That was a workers' neighborhood, the one that had supported Gaitán the most solidly at that time. . . .

Castro: When they saw the doors of the stores open, many poor and oppressed people looted. That's an objective, historical fact that can't be denied.

I realized that we had a large force of between 400 and 500 armed men holed up, on the defensive, and I asked for a chance to speak with the head of the garrison. Several officers were there. I said, "History shows that a force that is kept in barracks is lost." Cuba's experience of armed struggle shows that every troop that was kept in barracks was lost. I suggested that he take the troops into the street and assign them an attack mission, to seize objectives against the government. I argued with him, urging that he send the troops out to attack. They were strong and were capable of carrying out decisive actions; meanwhile, as long as they were kept there, they were lost. I presented my point of view and backed it up. He was kind enough to listen to me, but he did not make any decision. So I went back to my post.

I probably did that several times, urging that he take the troops out in the street and try to take the Palace and some other objective. I had developed my military ideas from my studies of the history of revolutions, of the popular movements that arose during the French Revolution and the storming of the Bastille, such as the mobilization of the people from the neighborhoods; and also from Cuba's own experience. I saw clearly that what he was doing was crazy. What happened? The army had apparently taken a stand in support of the government. The police were simply waiting for the government's forces to attack.

We spent all night waiting for the army to attack — all night. Every 15 minutes, someone would shout: "Here comes the attack!" And everybody would take up a protected position at the windows. Some tanks went by two or three times; the men shot at them, and the tanks fired machine guns at the building.

I made several fruitless attempts to convince the officer to go out into the streets.

Maybe around midnight or 1:00 in the morning an incident occurred that I still remember. The Liberals found a certain policeman and tied and beat him on the floor where I was. I was disgusted. They called him a *godo* [Conservative Party supporter] "He's a *godo*! He was in the police unit assigned to the OAS conference — look at his socks!" They were the socks and other clothes that were given to the policemen who had been working at the conference. They insulted him and beat him several times. I didn't like that.

During the night while we waited for an attack I thought of Cuba, of my family and everyone, and I felt very alone. There I was with my rifle and a few bullets. I asked myself, "What am I doing here? I've lost contact with everybody — with the students and the chief of police. Here I am in a mouse trap; this is completely wrong. It's wrong to sit here waiting for an attack instead of going out to attack with this force to carry out decisive actions." I started to wonder if I should leave. But I decided to stay. Handing the rifle to one of the men who did not have a weapon would have been the easy way out.

Then I was overcome by an internationalist sentiment. I thought: "Well, the people here are the same as the people in Cuba, the same as people everywhere. These people are oppressed and exploited." I argued to myself: "Their main leader has been assassinated and this uprising is absolutely justified. I may die here, but I'm staying." I made my decision knowing that it was a military disaster; that those people were going to lose; that I was alone; and that these were Colombians, not Cubans. However, I reasoned that people were the same everywhere, that their cause was just and that it was my duty to stay. So I stayed all night, waiting until dawn for an attack.

When I looked at the military situation, I saw that we were lost. The divisional headquarters was on a slope, with a hill and then Monserrate Hill behind it. I approached the commander again, and I told him that if the enemy attacked the fortress from above, we were lost. I told him that we should control the heights that were behind us. I asked for a patrol with which I could hold the heights. He gave me a small squad of about seven or eight men; so off I went with my patrol and took possession of the hills between the divisional headquarters and Monserrate Hill. My mission was to take the heights; I was expecting an attack. I spent the next day [April 10] patrolling the heights between Monserrate Hill and the divisional police headquarters.

Several things happened. I went a little farther south, patrolling to see if enemy troops were coming from that direction. At one time, I saw a car turning the corner of a street. I ordered it to stop, but it didn't; it kept on. I did not trust it. I ran and climbed to a higher place at the curve, to see better. After the car had gone around the curve, I heard a loud noise — it had crashed. The driver threw himself out of the car and took off running. I called on him to halt; but he did not stop. I didn't shoot, because I saw that he was not armed, but I imagined he was a spy.

There were several huts on the hill, and everybody had wine, food, lots of things. They had been supplied the day before. Everybody was very friendly, offering food, wine, everything they had. All the farmers who were on the heights where I was patrolling were very friendly. There were very few houses there then — perhaps 14 or 15 isolated huts in all. I visited several of the farmers' huts.

Do you know what the man I thought was a spy was doing? You won't believe it. I found out later from the local people when I asked if they had seen the man there. The city was burning, there was a cloud of smoke and you could hear shooting all over, but that man had taken two prostitutes from the city and had gone to those hills to have a good time. The farmers told me: "He's screwing! He's screwing two prostitutes." I had never heard that word before.

Later, three planes flew over us. We did not know whose side they were on. There was always hope, not knowing if the planes were with the revolution or with the government. The three planes flew around and around but did not do anything.

We spent the day there, and I shot a couple of times at the Ministry of War which I could see from my position. And, still, there was no army and no troops.

Alape: Did anybody return your fire?

Castro: No, because the Ministry was around 700 or 800 meters away, below us. It was the only target within range of my rifle.

There was one serious conflict, the only serious problem we had. It was around 4:00 p.m. when, suddenly, I saw some men coming from the divisional headquarters with a submachine gun and some sticks. I asked what was going on. They said that the Fifth Divisional Headquarters was being attacked. I urged them not to leave, saying that we should go there, that they shouldn't abandon the others. While I was arguing with them, they suddenly aimed the gun at me and nearly fired. They nearly killed me. I was trying to persuade them, but they were panicky and determined to leave. After they aimed their submachine gun at me they left.

Since the divisional headquarters was apparently under attack, I took the patrol down the hill; but there was no attack. To the contrary, a patrol had left the divisional headquarters and headed toward a building where some marksmen were holed up in a tower. I went with them. We went through the streets of a very poor neighborhood. First of all, we found a series of brick factories, kilns and tile works. I remember a little boy came up to me. His father had been killed by a stray bullet, and the boy choked out, as if asking me for help, "They've killed my dad! They've killed my dad!" He was only six or seven years old, and he was crying. The body of a civilian was lying in the middle of one street. We went toward the tower and the shooting stopped. We then returned to divisional headquarters. I spent my second night (April 10) there.

By the dawn of April 11, there was a lot of talk about an agreement between the government and the opposition forces. I still had my rifle and also a sword, a cutlass. I don't know where I got it. I had around nine bullets and my police greatcoat, my militiaman's beret (the cap without a visor) and the sword.

People were chatting, the men relaxed, and somebody addressed the troops about a peace agreement. They asked for the policemen to stay in the barracks, for the rifles to be turned in and for the civilians to go home. Everyone had treated me very well since I had arrived; perhaps they were glad to see the Cuban there with them, ready to fight; that made a good impression on them.

When the time came to leave in the morning, I wanted to take a souvenir — perhaps the sword — but they said no, not even that.

Betrayal

In fact, there was no agreement. It was a terrible act of betrayal; I think the people were betrayed. They talked to the people about having come to an agreement, but it wasn't so.

I turned my rifle in at about midday on the 11th. Another Cuban came by and told me about everything he had gone through; it was a miracle he hadn't been killed. He had been with the same division. At around midday, we walked toward the hotel. We went calmly, because peace had been restored, with a national agreement. However, as we approached the hotel, we saw that there was still shooting. Many revolutionaries — isolated snipers — were being hunted down one by one. A lot of fighters were killed.

The agreement was not based on justice and gave the people no guarantees. After an agreement was reached and the revolutionaries laid down their weapons, the army began hunting them down throughout the city.

When we reached the hotel, we found that we Cubans were being blamed for everything. Everyone asked, "What are you doing here? Everybody's been looking for you," and "Are you the Cubans?" We were notorious. There were some Conservatives in the hotel, too, and they were claiming that we were responsible for everything that had happened. There we were — without a cent, not having any friend's address, not knowing where to go. Imagine! It was around 2:00 or 3:00 p.m.

We went into the street. The snipers and the army were still fighting. We went to the rooming house where Ovares, the president of the FEU, and Guevara were. The owners of the house greeted us and promised to put us up as there was a curfew at 6:00 p.m.

I was full of everything I had seen; I was quite excited. Firstly,

Gaitán's assassination, and then the fighting, the people who had rebelled; then all the tragic things that had happened: the agreement and the betrayal. But it just so happened that the owner of the rooming house was a Conservative. When we arrived there, we were in civilian clothes and had no weapons. The owner began to say terrible things about Gaitán and the Liberals. I lost my patience and made a mistake as this was a little after 5:30, not long before the curfew. I told him he was wrong, that the people were oppressed and were struggling for a just cause. I got excited and argued with him, defending the people he was attacking. So he told us to leave.

I was really immature to make the mistake of arguing with the owner of the house just before the curfew. Leaving meant death. We walked out of the house and went to a hotel where many delegations were staying. I think it was the Granada, one of the two hotels. It was just five minutes before curfew time when I saw one of the Argentines I had met while organizing the congress — Iglesias, his name was — going by in a car with diplomatic license plates, one of those that had been used for the Pan American Conference. People were searching for the Cubans.

We stopped Iglesias's car and told him our problems. He said, "Get in!" So we did. He commented, "You've sure got yourselves in deep shit, *deep* shit. I'll take you to the Cuban Consulate." That's where he took us that night. We, who were enemies of the Cuban Government, were taken to the Cuban Consulate! Such are the paradoxes of history.

At 6:00, the curfew began. Everybody was armed to the teeth and checking all cars. They said, "Diplomatic? Go on! Diplomatic? Go on!" We got to the Cuban Consulate at around 6:10 p.m. We were already famous there, because everybody was looking for the Cubans, and they gave us a warm welcome. Do you know who the Consul was? A man around 65 years old. He looked very noble, and his wife was very sweet. That man, Tabernilla, was an elderly man who had spent his life in the diplomatic service, and was the kindest man you could imagine. His brother, an old military man, became a famous henchman of Batista's and head of Batista's army during our war.

That was the night of April 11. Because of what had happened, the Cuban Government had sent a military plane, and there were some military men there because there was a Cuban delegation at the Pan American Conference.

While we were there a lot of shooting broke out in front of the building; fresh from our experiences of the last 48 hours, we eagerly went out to see what was going on. The military men called us back inside saying, "No, no, not civilians." Those haughty military men, who had never heard any shooting in their lives, did not want us to see the shooting in front of the consulate. But the Consul gave us his full protection, welcoming and taking care of us.

We told him that there were two other Cubans in the city, and he sent a diplomatic car to the rooming house where the two other Cubans were and brought them back. So the four of us were together. The consulate fixed our papers, and we returned to Cuba on April 12 in a plane that had been sent to Colombia to get some bulls for a bullfight.

I took all the documents — the "Prayer for Peace" and all the other materials that Gaitán had given me. I had retrieved them from the hotel before leaving. We reached Cuba in the evening, after making a stopover in Baranquilla.

Lessons of the Bogotazo experience

That is how a series of near miracles ended. Above all, if we hadn't made it to the Granada Hotel at 5:55, we would have been killed; if we had been caught, we would have been blamed for everything. The government was trying to say it was all a communist plot whipped up by foreigners. The truth is that we had nothing to do with it. As young, idealistic, Don Quixote-like students, we simply joined in the people's rebellion.

Alape: Of all those experiences, what influenced you the most?

Castro: Well, I'll tell you. I already had revolutionary ideas; I wouldn't say that they were as completely formed as they are now. My theoretical ideas weren't as solidly based as they became some years later. In that period, I was already a supporter of Puerto Rican independence, Dominican democracy and the other key Latin American causes. I took part in the anti-imperialist struggle, and I wanted Latin American unity, the unity of our peoples against oppression and domination by the United States. I had already studied the basics of Marxism-Leninism, but I could not say that I was a Marxist-Leninist at that time, much less a member of the Communist Party or even of the Communist Youth.

Even much later, when I developed a revolutionary strategy backed by Marxist-Leninist training, I did not join the Communist

Party; rather, I created a new organization and acted as a member of it. It wasn't that I had any prejudices against the Communist Party; rather, I realized that the Communist Party was very isolated and that it would be very difficult to carry out my revolutionary plan from within its ranks. That's why I had to choose: to become a disciplined member of the Communist Party or to create a revolutionary organization that could act in Cuban conditions. By April 1948, I already had leftist ideas — above all, democratic, patriotic, anti-imperialist, populist ideas.

What was I in 1948? I was almost — but not quite — a communist. I had what was close to communist political concepts, but I was still influenced by the ideas of the French Revolution — above all, by the people's struggles, tactics and especially the military aspects.

Alape: Did the April events influence you in your revolutionary development?

Castro: The opportunity of seeing an absolutely spontaneous people's revolution must have had a great influence on me. It reaffirmed some ideas and concepts I already had about the exploited masses, the oppressed, the people seeking justice, like an erupting volcano. The people were oppressed, exploited and hungry. The death of Gaitán — who clearly offered the Colombian people hope — was what set off that explosion, which nobody organized and nobody could have organized; it was entirely spontaneously.

As always, imperialism and the oligarchy took advantage of the situation to say that it was the result of a communist conspiracy against the [OAS] conference. The congress that we were organizing against the conference had no links with the Communist Party of Cuba.

Alape: Was there any relationship between the April 9 uprising and the [1953] attack on the Moncada garrison?

Castro: It formed part of the experience I had had prior to the revolutionary struggle in Cuba. I knew at the time we attacked the Moncada that it was a very hard thing to do — not only because of what I had seen on April 9 but also because of other factors; I had made a serious study of the history of peoples' revolutions. By the time of the Moncada attack, I had matured and assimilated a lot of Marxism-Leninism, which I hadn't done before I went to Bogotá. I hadn't had that Marxist-Leninist training and did not have socialist convictions back then. Naturally, I was in a highly stimulating environment for developing my ideas. I had progressed and advanced a lot in my political viewpoint and had a progressive political outlook, but I did not yet have the political maturity and the depth of Marxist-Leninist social convictions that I had by the time of the Moncada attack.

In those days, I was greatly influenced by populist ideas, the ideas of the French Revolution, the ideas of struggling for our independence, the ideas of peoples' revolutions. Above all, I felt tremendous solidarity with the people, great fellow feeling with the people and tremendous hatred of oppression, injustice, poverty — all that.

I was 21 at the time, and I think I behaved pretty well. I feel proud of what I did. I maintained a consistent attitude. I reacted to Gaitán's death with the same indignation as the Colombians, and I reacted to the injustice and oppression that existed in that country just as the Colombians did, with great decision and selflessness. I think that I reacted with a lot of common sense, too, when I did everything possible to help organize things. If I were to give any advice now — at my age and with all the experience I have — I think it wouldn't be any better than the advice I gave in the Fifth Divisional Police Headquarters that night. I think that my decision to stay there, even though I was alone and it seemed to me that they were making a terrible tactical mistake that night, was proof of my selflessness and Quixote-like idealism. I remained loyal throughout. On the afternoon of the 10th, when I was told that the divisional headquarters was being attacked and that the police were deserting, I went to the divisional headquarters with my patrol. That is, my behavior was impeccable. I was disciplined.

Why did I stay, knowing it was suicidal and that they were making military mistakes? Because I had a sense of honor, idealism, a moral principle. That night the tanks kept going by and an attack was expected every half hour. I knew that, if an attack came, everybody there was going to die because it was a real mouse trap. And, even though I disagreed completely with what they were doing from the military point of view, I stayed. I was going to die there anonymously, but I stayed. I'm proud of that; I acted in accord with my moral principles, with dignity and honor, with discipline and with incredible selflessness. You had to see all the things that were happening there to appreciate this. Even my last Quixote-like act of arguing with the owner of the rooming house — an action which nearly cost me my life — was simply because I could not remain silent in view of what he said. Remember that I was 21 years old. With a little more experience, I might have shut up and let that Conservative say whatever he wanted and not have caused the situation from which we miraculously escaped. If we had been captured, they would have blamed everything on us, and I would not be here now telling you what really happened during the April 9 uprising.

The people demonstrated tremendous courage. What impressed me? Firstly, the phenomenon of how an oppressed people could erupt. Secondly, the courage and heroism of the Colombian people that I saw that day. However, there was no organization, no political education to accompany that heroism. There was political awareness and a rebellious spirit, but no political education and no leadership.

The April 9 uprising influenced me greatly in my later revolutionary life: having seen what happened then I made a tremendous effort to create political awareness and political education in Cuba. I wanted to avoid the revolution sinking into anarchy, looting, disorder and people taking the law into their own hands. The greatest influence those events had on me was in Cuba's revolutionary strategy, the idea of educating the people during our struggle so there wouldn't be any anarchy or looting when the revolution triumphed, and the people would not take revenge.

I had no precise ideas about all this back then, but later on I wondered whether, in similar circumstances, our people would have done exactly the same thing. I may be wrong, but I think our people had a little more political education; it would have been a little more difficult for the Cuban people, in a similar situation, to have engaged in looting instead of throwing themselves into revolutionary struggle — perhaps because they weren't as poor or economically desperate as the Colombians.

In Bogotá, many of the people — the poor people, the workers and students — engaged in combat, but almost everybody else, including some of the poor people, started looting. Not all of the poor people looted; many of them fought, but there were others who looted. That's the simple, unvarnished truth. Naturally, that's bad, because the oligarchs — who supported the status quo and wanted to portray the people as an anarchic, disorderly mob — took advantage of that situation. That influenced me a great deal — at least, in my becoming aware of the need to educate the people and draw political guidelines so there would not be any anarchy or looting and the people would not take justice into their own hands.

I also think that the Bogotá experience led me to identify more with the cause of the peoples. That oppressed people were fighting and struggling influenced me greatly from the point of view of my revolutionary feelings. I grieved over Gaitán's death; I felt the exploited, bloodied people's pain, the pain of the people who were defeated. I saw what imperialism, the oligarchy and the reactionary classes were capable of. Above all, I felt the pain of the betrayal. The people were betrayed, because they were told that there had been an agreement, a truce — which they supposed meant a change in the situation, an end to the bloodshed and guarantees for all. I'll never forget how, after the agreement, after the truce, after they had turned in their weapons, dozens of revolutionaries were hunted down in the city. They were heroes. How courageous the snipers were! There they were, fighting alone, with no information, and fighting on.

Role of Communist Party

The Communist Party had nothing to do with it. I think that the leftists, including both Liberals and Communists, fought alongside the people — all the people fought. But it was a lie to say the Colombian Communist Party, the Cuban Communist Party or the international communist movement was responsible for the uprising; that was just one more lie that was told.

The Communist Party had very few members in that period; it was small. The Liberal Party was the main political force, especially in the universities and among the poor. Nobody organized the uprising. I'm positive about this, because the uprising was spontaneous among the people. The violence with which the people reacted shows how oppressed they were and how much Gaitán meant to them. His assassination meant the death of hope. It was the last straw. And, simply, the people erupted. I saw that immediately. The people in the street, the ordinary people, ran around shouting, furious — *furious*. It was the most incredible outbreak you can imagine: the oppressed, hungry people, who had no political awareness, were unorganized and had no leadership.

Many of the police joined the uprising, and the army hesitated. There was support for Gaitán among the military. They had followed

Cortés's trial with great interest, and there was support for Gaitán. The army hesitated, but the masses weren't organized and had no leadership or enough political education. Then, at the moment of seizing power, part of the people set about solving immediate problems: getting things, food or whatever. In fact, there was chaos, anarchy and looting. It had a negative effect. There's no doubt about this; it's a fact: there was looting — I saw people looting. They weren't organized. If there had been a few capable leaders, the April 9 uprising would have ended in a people's victory.

The betrayal made a terrible lasting impression on me. I think that the Liberal Party leaders betrayed the people — simply that — they betrayed the people. They weren't capable of leading the people, of taking Gaitán's place, and weren't loyal to the people. They made an unprincipled agreement because they feared revolution.

How did this relate to our experience on July 26 [1953 assault at Moncada]? I continued my revolutionary political development, building on what I was at that time. But few times in my life have I been as selfless and pure as I was during those days. In my subsequent life as a revolutionary, I think that I have acted in the same way as I did on that night: when I examined my conscience and asked myself what I was doing there, (even though I considered that they were wrong militarily), that it was not my homeland and that I was alone. Despite all that, I decided to stay. That's what I have done ever since, throughout my life. I have always reacted that way. I feel proud of my behavior in those days. My presence was an accident as our congress had nothing to do with what happened. Our congress was to protest against imperialism, against the OAS. In fact, the uprising frustrated the organization of the congress.

Alape: Did you have any problems on your return to Cuba?

Castro: No. It was known that some Cubans had been there, but it wasn't given much importance. The thing is, the Cubans had been blamed for everything that happened there. The Cubans' presence was used by those who wanted to make it seem that it was all a plot by international Communism and that the Cubans had organized it all. The presence of the Cubans was used to blame a few foreigners for everything that had happened. The two Cubans weren't at all to blame for what had happened; the Cubans simply joined in. I joined a people's uprising — because that was my calling and because of my principles and revolutionary solidarity.

4

Preparing for Moncada

I already had acquired a Marxist outlook when we attacked the Moncada military garrison. I had fairly well-developed revolutionary ideas, acquired while I was at the university through my contact with revolutionary literature.

It is a curious thing: as a result of studying capitalist political economy, I started drawing socialist conclusions and imagining a society whose economy would operate more rationally. This was before I discovered Marxist literature. I started off as a utopian communist. I did not come in contact with revolutionary ideas, revolutionary theories, the *Communist Manifesto* and the first works by Marx, Engels and Lenin until I was a junior in the university. To be quite frank, the simplicity, clarity and direct manner in which our world and society are explained in the *Communist Manifesto* had a particularly significant impact on me.

Naturally, before becoming a utopian or a Marxist communist, I was a follower of José Martí; I mustn't omit that. I have been a supporter of Martí's ideas ever since I was in high school. Martí's ideas impressed all of us and we really admired him. Also, I always wholeheartedly identified with our people's heroic struggles for independence in the past century.

I've spoken to you about the Bible, but I could also tell you about our country's extremely interesting history, which is filled with

---

From Frei Betto's interview with Fidel Castro in May 1985, published as Fidel and Religion *by Ocean Press.*

examples of courage, dignity and heroism. Just as the Church has its martyrs and heroes, so too the history of any country; it is almost like a religion. My heart was always filled with something like veneration when I listened to the story of General Antonio Maceo, the "bronze titan," who waged so many battles and performed so many feats; or when I was told about Ignacio Agramonte; or Máximo Gómez, that great Dominican internationalist and brilliant military commander who fought on the Cuban side from the beginning; or the innocent medical students who were shot in 1871 for allegedly having desecrated a Spaniard's grave. We heard a lot about Martí and Carlos Manuel de Céspedes, the father of this country.

So together with biblical history, there was another history that we considered sacred: our country's history, the history of our nation's heroes. I got that not so much from the other members of my family — because they had not had much education — but from books I read at school. Gradually, I came in contact with other models of people and behavior.

Before becoming a Marxist, I was a great admirer of our country's history and of Martí. I was a disciple of Martí. Both Marx and Martí begin with an *M*, and I think they resemble each other greatly. I'm absolutely convinced that if Martí had lived in the same environment as Marx, he would have had the same ideas and acted in more or less the same way. Martí had great respect for Marx. He once said of him, "Since he sided with the weak, he deserves honor." When Marx died Martí wrote some very beautiful words about him.

I think that Martí's works contain such great and beautiful things that you can become a Marxist by taking his thought as a starting point. Of course, Martí did not explain why society was divided into classes, though he was a man who always stood on the side of the poor and who bitterly criticized the worst vices of a society of exploiters.

When I first got hold of the *Communist Manifesto* I found an explanation for many things. In the midst of a forest of events, where it was very difficult to understand anything and where everything seemed due to the wickedness of men — their defects, perversity and immorality — I started to identify other factors not dependent on the individual attitude and morals of men.

I began to understand human society, the historical process, and the divisions that I saw every day. After all, you don't need a map, a microscope or a telescope to see class divisions that mean that the poor go hungry while others have more than they need. Who could know this better than I, who had experienced both realities and who had even been, in part, a victim of the two? How could I fail to understand my experiences, the situation of the landowner and of the landless, barefoot farmer?

When I spoke to you about my father and Birán, I should have mentioned that although he was a big landowner, he was a very kind — an extremely kind — man. His political ideas, of course, were those of a landowner. He must have been aware of the conflict between his interests and those of the wage earner. Even so, he was a man who never said no to anyone who asked him for something, to anybody who came to him for help. That's very interesting.

My father's land was surrounded by latifundia owned by U.S. citizens. He owned large tracts of land, but they were surrounded by three big sugar mills, each of which had tens of thousands of hectares of land. One of them alone had over 120,000 hectares, and another, around 200,000. It was a chain of sugar mills. The U.S. owners had very strict standards for managing their property; they were ruthless. The owners did not live there but in New York. They had an administrator who was given a budget for expenses, and he could not spend a penny more.

During the dead season after the sugar harvest, many people used to come to our place. They spoke to my father, saying, "I've got such-and-such a problem; we're hungry; we need something, some help, some credit at the store," and so on. Those who did not usually work there would go to him and say, "We need work; give us work." My father's sugarcane fields were the cleanest in all of Cuba. While others had their fields weeded only once, my father organized three or four weedings, so as to give those people work. I can't recall his ever failing to find a solution whenever somebody came to him. Sometimes he grumbled and complained, but his generosity always got the upper hand. That was a characteristic of my father.

During my vacations I had to work. When I was an adolescent, my father used to take me to the office or have me work at the store. I had to spend part of my vacation working, which was not at all voluntary. I had no alternative. I'll never forget the many poor people who came there — barefoot, ragged and hungry — looking for a chit so they could buy something at the store. This was an oasis compared to the way the workers were treated on the U.S.-owned latifundia during the dead season.

By the time I started having revolutionary ideas and discovered Marxist literature, I had already had a very close look at the contrast between wealth and poverty, between a family with large tracts of land and those who had absolutely nothing. Who had to explain to me a society divided into classes and the exploitation of man by man to me, since I had seen it all with my own eyes and even suffered from it in a way?

If you already have certain rebellious traits, certain ethical values, and you come across an idea that gives you greater insight — such as the ones that helped me to understand the world and the society in which I lived, what I could see all around me — how can you fail to feel the impact of a veritable political revelation? I was deeply attracted to that literature; it completely won me over. Just as Ulysses was ensnared by the Sirens' songs, I was captivated by the irrefutable truths of Marxist literature. Immediately I began to grasp it, to understand and see things. Later on, many compatriots, who had no previous idea of these issues but who were honest people eager to end the injustices that existed in our country, also had that same experience. As soon as they were provided with some elements of Marxist theory, they felt the same impact.

Christian revolutionaries

Betto: Didn't this Marxist consciousness breed prejudices in you with regard to the Christian revolutionaries who joined the July 26 Movement — such as Frank País,[1] for example? What happened?

Castro: Let me tell you. Neither I nor any of the other comrades ever had any conflict — not that I can recall — with anyone over religious matters. As I told you, I already had a Marxist-Leninist outlook. I graduated from the university in 1950, and I had acquired a fully revolutionary outlook — not just in terms of ideas, but also in terms of purposes and how to implement them, how to apply it all to our country's conditions — in a very short period. I think that was very important.

---

[1] Frank País was a young revolutionary who sought to link the student movement in Oriente province with the struggles of workers and peasants. He played a leading role in the underground movement until he was captured and murdered in July 1957 by Batista's forces.

When I enrolled in the university, I first became involved with an opposition party that was very critical of political corruption, embezzlement and fraud.

Betto: The Orthodox Party?

Castro: Yes. Its official name was the Cuban People's Party, and it had broad mass support. Many well-meaning, honest people belonged to that party. The main emphasis was placed on criticizing corruption, embezzlement, abuse and injustice, constantly denouncing Batista's abuses during his previous term. This was linked at the university to a tradition of struggle, including the martyrs of the School of Medicine in 1871 and the struggles against Machado and Batista. Also during that period, the university took a stand against the Grau San Martín administration, because of its fraud and embezzlement and the frustrations it caused the country.

Like many other young people at the university, I had already established relations with that party almost at the beginning, before I had any contact with the Marxist literature I was telling you about. When I graduated, my ties with the party were very strong, but my ideas had developed much farther.

After graduation, I wanted to take some graduate courses. I was aware that I needed more training before devoting myself fully to politics. I especially wanted to study political economy. I had made a great effort at the university to pass the courses that would enable me to obtain degrees in law, diplomatic law and social sciences, in order to get a scholarship. I was already living on my own; my family gave me some help during the first few years, but by the time I finished college — I was even married by then— I could not think of continuing to receive help from my family. Even so I wanted to study, and the only way to do it was by getting a scholarship abroad. To obtain that scholarship, I had to get those three degrees. The scholarship was already within my reach. I had to take only two more courses out of the 50 I had to pass in two years. No other student in my class had done this, so there was no competition. But then impatience and my contact with reality forced me to act. I did not have the three years I needed to continue my studies, the ones I needed to study economics and improve and deepen my theoretical knowledge.

Rather well equipped with the main ideas and with a revolutionary outlook, I then decided to put them into practice. Before the coup d'état of March 10, 1952, I already had a revolutionary outlook and even an idea of how to implement it. When I entered the university, I had no revolutionary culture yet. Less than eight years passed between the development of that outlook and the triumph of the revolution in Cuba.

I've said that I had no mentor. The effort to think through, develop and apply those ideas in such a short time was very great. What I had learned of Marxism-Leninism was decisive in this. I believe that my contribution to the Cuban revolution consists of having synthesized Martí's ideas and those of Marxism-Leninism and of having applied them consistently in our struggle.

I saw that the Cuban Communists were isolated due to the enveloping atmosphere of imperialism, McCarthyism and reactionary politics. No matter what they did they remained isolated. They had managed to become strong within the labor movement; a large number of party members had worked with the Cuban working class, devoting themselves to the workers, and had done a great deal for them and won great prestige among them; but I did not see any political possibilities for them under those circumstances.

So, I worked out a revolutionary strategy for carrying out a deep social revolution — but gradually, by stages. I basically decided to carry it out with the broad, rebellious, discontented masses, who did not have a mature political consciousness of the need for revolution but who constituted the immense majority of the people. I said, "The rebellious masses, the untainted, ordinary people, are the force that can make the revolution, the decisive factor in the revolution. They must be led to revolution, but they must be led by stages." Such a consciousness could not be created overnight with mere words. It was clear to me that the masses were the basic factor — the still-confused masses in many cases, prejudiced against socialism and communism; the masses who had received no real political education, influenced as they were from all quarters by the mass media and everything: radio, television, movies, books, magazines, newspapers and reactionary antisocialist preaching everywhere.

Socialism and communism were depicted as the enemies of humanity. This was one of the arbitrary, unfair uses made of the mass media in our country, one of the methods used by the reactionary social forces in Cuba, like everywhere else. Very early in life, you'd hear that socialism meant denying one's homeland, depriving farmers of their land and people of their personal property, dividing families, and so on. In Marx's time, socialism was accused of introducing the community of women — a charge that was given a devastating rebuttal by the great socialist thinker. The most horrible, most absurd things were invented to poison the people against revolutionary ideas. Many people who were part of the masses might be anticommunist; beggars, hungry people and the unemployed might be anticommunist. They did not know what communism or socialism was all about. However, I could see that the masses were suffering from poverty, injustice, humiliation and inequality. The people's suffering wasn't just material; it was moral, as well. You don't suffer just because you're getting 1,500 calories and you need 3,000. There's another sort of suffering, too — social inequality, which makes you feel constantly debased and humiliated as a human being, because you're treated like dirt, as if you did not exist, as if you are nothing.

Then I realized that the masses were decisive, that the masses were extremely angry and discontented. They did not understand the social essence of the problem; they were confused. They attributed unemployment, poverty, and the lack of schools, hospitals, job opportunities and housing — almost everything — to administrative corruption, embezzlement and the perversity of the politicians.

The Cuban People's Party had harnessed much of that discontent, but it did not blame the capitalist system and imperialism for it very much. I would say that this was because we had been taught a third religion: the religion of respect for and gratitude to the United States. "The United States gave us our independence. It is our friend; it helped us and is still helping us." This appeared quite frequently in official texts.

I'm trying to explain a historical reality. We were told "independence began on May 20, 1902," the day when the United States handed us a neocolonial republic with a constitutional amendment that gave it the right to intervene in Cuba. By the way, May 20 was the day they chose for initiating the broadcasts of Radio Goebbels, Radio Reagan, Radio Hitler — I'm not going to call that subversive radio station "Radio Martí."[2] When the United States imposed the Platt amendment on Cuba, it had already been occupying our territory for four years. It occupied the country for

---

[2] U.S. government radio broadcast to Cuba which commenced in 1985.

four years and then imposed its infamous right to intervene in our country. It intervened more than once and seized our best land, our mines, our trade, our finances and our economy.

It started in 1898 and culminated on May 20, 1902, with a caricature of a republic, the political expression of the U.S. colony established in Cuba. That was when the massive appropriation of Cuba's natural resources and wealth began. I told you about my father, who worked for a famous U. S. company, the United Fruit Company, which was established in the northern part of Oriente Province. My father was a United Fruit worker. That's where he started working in Cuba.

Textbooks praised the American way of life, and they were complemented by all sorts of literature. Now even the children know that all that was a great big lie. How do you go about destroying all those lies, all those myths? How do you destroy them? I remember that the people knew nothing, but they suffered. The people were confused, but they were also desperate and able to fight and to move in a given direction. The people had to be led to the road of revolution by stages, step by step, until they achieved full political consciousness and confidence in their future.

I worked out all those ideas by reading and studying Cuban history, the Cuban personality and distinguishing characteristics, and Marxism.

Betto: Were you in the left wing of the Orthodox Party?

Castro: Some people knew what I thought and some were already trying to block me. They called me a communist, because I explained everything to everyone rather candidly. But I was not preaching socialism as the immediate objective at that time. I spoke out against injustice, poverty, unemployment, high rent, the eviction of farmers, low wages, political corruption and ruthless exploitation everywhere. This was a denunciation, a preaching, and a program for which our people were much better prepared and where I had to start working in order to lead the people in a really revolutionary direction.

I noticed that even though it was strong and had influence among the workers, the Communist Party was isolated. I saw it as a potential ally. Of course, I could not have convinced a Communist Party member of the fact that my theories were right. I did not even try to do that. What I did was to pursue those ideas after I already had a Marxist-Leninist outlook. I had a very good relationship with them.

Almost all of the books I read were bought on credit at the Communist Party bookstore on Carlos III Street. I also had a very good relationship with Communist leaders at the university; we were allies in almost every struggle. But I would think, "There is a possibility to work with the large, potentially revolutionary masses." I was putting those ideas into practice even before Batista's coup on March 10, 1952.

Betto: Did the members of the group that attacked the Moncada garrison belong to the left wing of the Orthodox Party?

Castro: They came from among the young people in that party whom I knew. I also knew how they thought. When the coup was staged, I started to organize them; I was organizing combat cells, I was setting up a military organization. I did not have an independent revolutionary plan as yet, because that was in the first few months after the 1952 military coup. I had had a long-term strategic plan since 1951, but it called for a preliminary political period.

Just after the coup I proposed a revolutionary movement. I even had some political strength. The Orthodox Party was set to win the election. I knew that its leadership in almost all the provinces — all except Havana Province — was already in the hands of the landowners and bourgeoisie, as was always the case. That party was virtually in the hands of the reactionary elements and electoral machines — except for Havana Province where a group of honest, prestigious politicians, intellectuals and university professors prevailed. There was no machine, though some rich people were trying to take control of the party in the province, using the traditional methods of machines and money.

The party was quite strong in Havana. It had 80,000 members who had joined spontaneously — that was a considerable number. It grew — especially after the death of its founder [Chibás], a militant man with great influence among the masses who killed himself as the result of a controversy with a government minister. He had charged the minister with having purchased property in Guatemala with embezzled funds, but he could not prove it. Even though corruption was rampant in the country, he fell into a trap, starting a controversy over that issue without being able to provide any concrete evidence. He grew desperate and committed suicide. The party was virtually without leadership, but it had enormous strength.

I was already saying that the [Orthodox] party was going to win the June 1952 presidential election. I also knew what was going to happen with that government: it would end up in frustration. However, I was already thinking of a preliminary political stage of preparing the movement and a second stage of seizing power in a revolutionary way. I think that one of the key things that Marxism taught me — and that I also knew intuitively — was that power had to be seized in order to make the revolution and that nothing could be accomplished through the traditional political methods.

I was thinking of using certain positions as a platform from which to launch a revolutionary program — initially, in the form of legislative bills — that later became the Moncada program. It was not a socialist program yet, but it could win the support of large masses of the population, and it was the first step toward socialism in Cuba. I had worked out the ideas of the Moncada program long before Batista's coup. I was already organizing a powerful base with poor shantytown dwellers in Havana and other poor sectors in the city and province. I also worked actively with Orthodox Party members.

Since I already was a lawyer, I had close contact with those sectors in an active, dynamic, energetic struggle, supported by the efforts of a small group of comrades. I did not hold any leadership posts, but I had broad mass support in that party and a revolutionary outlook. When the coup took place everything changed. It became impossible to carry out that initial program, in which I had included the soldiers, as I considered them to be victims of exploitation as they were put to work on the private farms of magnates, the president and the colonels. I could see all that, and I denounced it and even had some subtle influence among their ranks. At least they were interested in the denunciations. I planned to include in that movement: soldiers, workers, farmers, students, teachers, professionals and the middle class — all in a broad program.

When the coup took place, everything changed. As a first step, I thought we would have to go back to the previous constitutional stage. The military dictatorship would have to be defeated. I thought we would have to recover the country's previous status and that everybody would join forces to wipe out Batista's infamous, reactionary coup. I started to organize ordinary militant members of the Orthodox youth group on my own, and I also contacted some of the leaders of that party. I did this on my own. Some of the leaders said they favored armed struggle. I was sure that we would have to overthrow Batista by force of arms in order to return to the previous stage, to the constitutional regime, and I was convinced that that was the objective of all the parties. I had already worked out the first revolutionary strategy with a large mass movement that would be implemented initially through constitutional channels. I thought that everybody would unite to overthrow Batista's regime, including all those parties that had formed part of the government and all the opposition parties — everybody.

I began to organize the first combatants, the first fighters — the first cells — within a few weeks. First, I tried to set up a small, mimeographed newspaper and some underground radio stations. Those were the first things. We had some run-ins with the police that served as useful experience later on. When it came time to apply that experience, we were extremely careful in choosing cadres and in protecting the security of the organization. That's when we became true conspirators and started organizing the first nuclei for what we thought would be a united struggle by all the parties and all the other forces. That's how I began in that party, where I met a lot of earnest young people. I looked for them in the poorest sectors in Artemisa and Havana, among the workers, with several comrades who supported me right from the beginning: Abel Santamaría,[3] Jesús Montané, Ñico López[4] and some others — a very small group.

I became a professional cadre. At the beginning until just before the July 26, 1953, attack on the Moncada garrison, that movement had one professional cadre — me. Abel joined me a few days before the attack, so there were two cadres during the last month.

We organized that movement in just 14 months, and it came to have 1,200 people. I talked to every one of them and organized every cell, every group of the 1,200! Do you know how many kilometers I drove before the attack on the Moncada garrison? Forty thousand. All that effort was devoted to the organization, training and equipping of the movement. How many times I met with the future fighters, shared my ideas with them and gave them instructions!

By the way, the car we used hadn't been paid for. Since I was a

---

[3] Abel Santamaría was captured, tortured and murdered after the Moncada assault on July 26, 1953.
[4] Nico López was a founding member of the July 26 Movement who was captured and killed after landing with the *Granma* expedition in December 1956.

professional cadre and there were always bills outstanding, Abel and Montané supported me and paid for the car.

In this way, we created a disciplined organization with honest, determined young people who had patriotic, progressive ideas. Of course, we were organizing to fight the dictatorship. We did not intend to lead that struggle; we simply wanted to cooperate with all our forces. There were plenty of well-known political chiefs and personalities already. Then the stage came when we concluded that everything was a fraud, a falsehood and an impossibility. So we decided to work out our own plan. That changed everything.

Epilogue*

I am inspired by the grand spectacle of the great revolutions of history, because they have always signified the triumph of aims embodying the welfare and happiness of the vast majority as opposed to a tiny group of vested interests.

Do you know what episode really moves me? The revolution of the black slaves in Haiti. At a time when Napoleon was imitating Caesar and France resembled Rome, the soul of Spartacus was reborn in Toussaint L'Ouverture. How little importance is given to the fact that the African slaves who rebelled set up a free republic, defeating the greatest generals Napoleon had! It's true that Haiti has not progressed very much since then, but have the other Latin American republics done any better?

I keep thinking about these things, because, frankly, how pleased I would be to revolutionize this country from top to bottom! I am sure that all the people could be happy — and for them I would be ready to incur the hatred and ill will of a few thousand individuals, including some of my relatives, half of my acquaintances, two-thirds of my professional colleagues, and four-fifths of my former schoolmates.

---

* *From Fidel Castro's letter from prison, April 15, 1954*

Also published by Ocean Press

CHE GUEVARA READER
Writings on Guerrilla Strategy, Politics and Revolution
Edited by David Deutschmann
Three decades after the death of the legendary Latin American figure, this book presents the most comprehensive selection of Guevara's writings ever to be published in English. It includes an extensive chronology, glossary and a complete bibliography of Guevara's writings.
ISBN 1-875284-93-1

CHE GUEVARA AND THE FBI
U.S. political police dossier on the Latin American revolutionary
Edited by Michael Ratner and Michael Steven Smith
A Freedom of Information case succeeded in obtaining Che Guevara's FBI and CIA files, which are reproduced in this book. These sensational materials add to suspicions that U.S. spy agencies were plotting to assassinate Guevara in the 1960s.
ISBN 1-875284-76-1

CIA TARGETS FIDEL
The secret assassination report
Only recently declassified and published for the first time, this secret report was prepared for the CIA on its own plots to assassinate Cuba's Fidel Castro.
ISBN 1-875284-90-7

ZR RIFLE
The plot to kill Kennedy and Castro
by Claudia Furiati
Cuba finally opens its secret files on the assassination of President Kennedy, which show how and why the CIA, along with anti-Castro exiles and the Mafia, planned the conspiracy.
"Adds new pieces to the puzzle and gives us a clearer picture of what really happened." — Oliver Stone, director of "JFK".
ISBN 1-875284-85-0

THE SECRET WAR
CIA covert operations against Cuba, 1959-62
by Fabián Escalante
The secret war that the CIA lost. For the first time, the former head of Cuban State Security speaks out about the confrontation with U.S. spy agencies and presents stunning new evidence of the conspiracy between the Mafia, the Cuban counterrevolution and the CIA.
ISBN 1-875284-86-9

CUBA AND THE UNITED STATES
A Chronological History
by Jane Franklin
Based on exceptionally wide research, this updated and expanded chronology by U.S. historian Jane Franklin relates day by day, year by year, the developments involving the two neighboring countries from the 1959 Cuban revolution through 1995.
ISBN 1-875284-92-3

CUBA: TALKING ABOUT REVOLUTION
New, expanded edition
Conversations with Juan Antonio Blanco by Medea Benjamin
A frank discussion on the current situation in Cuba, this book presents an all-too-rare opportunity to hear the voice of one of the island's leading intellectuals. This expanded edition features a new chapter on "Cuba: 'socialist museum' or social laboratory?"
ISBN 1-875284-97-7

IN THE EYE OF THE STORM
Castro, Khrushchev, Kennedy and the Missile Crisis
by Carlos Lechuga
For the first time, Cuba's view of the most serious crisis of the Cold War is told by one of the leading participants.
ISBN 1-875284-87-7

FACE TO FACE WITH FIDEL CASTRO
A conversation with Tomás Borge
Issues facing a changing world are discussed in a lively dialogue between two of Latin America's most controversial political figures.
ISBN 1-875284-72-9

FIDEL AND RELIGION
Conversations with Frei Betto
A best-seller throughout Latin America in which Fidel Castro and liberation theologist Frei Betto discuss the church and politics.
ISBN 1-875284-05-2

CUBA AT THE CROSSROADS
by Fidel Castro
What future lies ahead for Cuba as it faces the new millennium? Must it now turn its back on the past four decades since the 1959 revolution? In a series of speeches over recent years, President Fidel Castro of Cuba discusses the main issues confronting the small Caribbean nation as it tries to adjust to a "new world order."
ISBN 1-875284-94-X

AFROCUBA
An anthology of Cuban writing on race, politics and culture
Edited by Pedro Pérez Sarduy and Jean Stubbs
What is it like to be Black in Cuba? Does racism exist in a revolutionary society that claims to have abolished it? *AfroCuba* looks at the Black experience in Cuba through the eyes of the island's writers, scholars and artists.
ISBN 1-875284-41-9

SLOVO
The unfinished autobiography of ANC leader Joe Slovo
A revealing and highly entertaining autobiography of one of the key figures of the African National Congress. As an immigrant, a Jew, a communist and guerrilla fighter — and white — few public figures in South Africa were as demonized by the apartheid government.
ISBN 1-875284-95-8

PRIEST AND PARTISAN
A South African journey of Father Michael Lapsley
by Michael Worsnip
The story of Father Michael Lapsley, an anti-apartheid priest who became the target of a South African letter bomb attack in 1990 in which he lost both hands and an eye.
ISBN 1-875284-96-6

CHE — A MEMOIR BY FIDEL CASTRO

Preface by Jesús Montané
Edited by David Deutschmann
For the first time Fidel Castro writes with candor and affection of his relationship with Ernesto Che Guevara, documenting his extraordinary bond with Cuba from the revolution's early days to the final guerrilla expeditions to Africa and Bolivia.
ISBN 1-875284-15-X

JOSE MARTI READER
Writings on the Americas
An outstanding new anthology of the writings, poetry and letters of José Martí — one of the most brilliant and impassioned Latin American intellectuals of the 19th century.
ISBN 1-875284-12-5

PSYWAR ON CUBA
The declassified history of U.S. anti-Castro propaganda
by Jon Elliston
Secret CIA and U.S. Government documents are published here for the first time, showing a 40-year campaign by Washington to use psychological warfare and propaganda to destabilize Cuba.
ISBN 1-876175-09-5

CHE IN AFRICA
Che Guevara's Congo Diary
by William Gálvez
Che in Africa is the previously untold story of Che Guevara's "lost year" in Africa. Che Guevara disappeared from Cuba in 1965 to lead a guerrilla mission to Africa in support of liberation movements. The story behind the Congo mission is now revealed, reprinting Guevara's previously unpublished Congo Diary.
ISBN 1-876175-08-7

Ocean Press
Australia: GPO Box 3279, Melbourne 3001, Australia
  ● Fax: 61-3-9372 1765 ● E-mail: ocean_press@msn.com
USA: PO Box 834, Hoboken, NJ 07030, USA
  ● Fax: 1-201-617 0203